MAN.

Today's business organizations, especially large ones, are complex places; difficult to manage and to control. Much of this complexity is self-induced and too much of the management of these organizations is done on an ad hoc basis. Different reporting, control and management systems are used in different parts of the company and often these are incompatible, making it difficult, sometimes impossible for top management to know what is going on. Consequently it is an arduous task for managers to make strategic plans for the business or react quickly to changes in the environment.

This book shows how much of this complexity can be smoothed away through the introduction of overarching management frameworks that are complete, consistent and comprehensive, bringing all the various parts of the organization together as a single system. It provides a whole-firm view of management and suggests that reputational and ethical issues are equally important to marketing, operations and finance and need to be considered within the framework.

Management Frameworks is a practical and insightful book, offering students the tools and knowledge required for viewing strategy and management holistically. It will be required reading for executive education classes in strategic management and will find a ready audience with thinking managers everywhere.

Jacques Kemp worked for ING on all continents in various executive positions. Presently he is sharing his experiences and insights as a board and council member for a wide range of organizations. He also counsels young entrepreneurs and guest-lectures at MBA programs.

Andreas Schotter is Professor of Strategy at Thunderbird School of Global Management, USA and has twice been named a Wall Street Journal Distinguished Professor of the Year. Before embarking on an academic career, he was a senior executive with several multinational corporations in Europe, Asia, Australia and North America.

Morgen Witzel is a Fellow of the Centre for Leadership Studies, University of Exeter, UK. A writer, lecturer and consultant on business and management, especially on the history of management, he is the author of eighteen books and hundreds of articles for the academic and popular press.

MANAGEMENT FRAMEWORKS

Aligning strategic thinking and execution

*Jacques Kemp, Andreas Schotter
and Morgen Witzel*

Routledge
Taylor & Francis Group

LONDON AND NEW YORK

First published 2013
by Routledge
2 Park Square, Milton Park, Abingdon, Oxon OX14 4RN

Simultaneously published in the USA and Canada
by Routledge
711 Third Avenue, New York, NY 10017

Routledge is an imprint of the Taylor & Francis Group, an informa business

British Library Cataloguing in Publication Data
A catalogue record for this book is available from the British Library

Library of Congress Cataloging in Publication Data
   Kemp, Jacques.
   Management frameworks: aligning strategic thinking and execution /
Jacques Kemp, Andreas Schotter, and Morgen Witzel.
       p. cm.
   Includes bibliographical references and index.
   1. Strategic planning. 2. Management. 3. Organizational change.
   I. Schotter, Andreas. II. Witzel, Morgen. III. Title.
   HD30.28.K455 2012
   658.4′012—dc23
                                                              2012015532
ISBN: 978–0–415–78164–0 (hbk)
ISBN: 978–0–415–78165–7 (pbk)
ISBN: 978–0–203–08489–2 (ebk)

Typeset in Bembo
by RefineCatch Limited, Bungay, Suffolk

Printed and bound in Great Britain by the MPG Books Group

CONTENTS

ILLUSTRATIONS

Figures

Boxes

ACKNOWLEDGEMENTS

A great many people have commented on the ideas in this book or otherwise influenced its development over the course of time. We would all like to thank our professional colleagues, who have been a tremendous source of inspiration. In particular thanks must go to Bob Epner for his kind permission to reproduce the illustrations from his original article.

Others who must be singled out for especial thanks include Professor Rod White and Professor Paul W. Beamish from the Richard Ivey School of Business at the University of Western Ontario, Professor Gao Xudong of Tsinghua University, Beijing, Professor Dam Cho of Chonnam National University, Korea, Professor Mark Zmijewski of the University of Chicago, Professor Anthony Hourihan of University College Dublin, Assistant Professor Brian Tjemkes of the Vrije Universiteit, Amsterdam, Associate Professor Jan Willem Stoelhorst and Associate Professor Willemijn van Dolen of Universiteit van Amsterdam, Associate Professor Will Felps of the Rotterdam School of Management (Erasmus), and Associate Professor Huub Ruel of the University of Twente. Special thanks to Mr Alexander Rinnooy Kan, formerly of ING, who was very supportive of the development of the TPE framework at ING Asia/Pacific and other ING units.

We would also like to extend our thanks to Terry Clague, our helpful and understanding commissioning editor at Routledge, and to all the team there who brought this book to publication.

JK
AS
MW

1

TOO COMPLEX TO MANAGE?

> The aim of Occupy is not to think for yourself . . . We want to change the process of finding solutions.
>
> *(Maria, Occupy protestor at the World Economic Forum, Davos, 2012)*

In an increasingly complex world, leaders and managers must cope with many unexpected issues and unforeseen events. This of course increases business risks, but it also creates potential new opportunities. Adaptability, especially the personal and organizational capability to reconfigure quickly and efficiently, has become the key to achieving superior performance.

Few public or private organizations have been able to develop the internal capabilities to adapt the core elements of their organizational cultures and mindset of their managers. In this chapter, we will describe how complexities seem to keep multiplying at an ever-increasing pace. We will also show how many of our personal capabilities are severely constrained by 'silo' approaches to management and by the lack of skills and processes that are needed to 'connect all the dots' in order to manage in an integrated but dynamic way.

The solution to the problem lies in the introduction of overarching management frameworks into the management process. These frameworks should involve all key decision-makers in all business units and functions. The results of the introduction of frameworks can be far-reaching. They can result in enhanced understanding and better social cohesion within the organization, and hence more *organizational alignment*. They can assist us in managing complexities, which should in turn lead to greater efficiency. A well organized approach to management – in other words, the better 'management of management', can help to reduce the creeping inefficiencies of large and complex organizations, often referred to as 'corporate discount', and turn these instead into a 'corporate premium'. Through simplified, streamlined, holistic management frameworks, organizations can avoid the problem of becoming *too complex to manage*.

Let us look at a couple of prominent examples, where well-known, successful organizations have experienced serious crises because of the lack of efficient management frameworks.

January 24, 2008. French financial group Société Générale announced the loss of €4.9 billion due to the actions of a rogue trader. The trader, Jérôme Kerviel, was accused of having set up a string of fake deals in order to defraud the bank. Arrested and charged with several offences, he was convicted in October 2010, but the money was never recovered.

Like other similar incidents, such as the actions of rogue trader Nick Leeson who brought down Barings Bank in 1995, no one in a top leadership role at Société Générale was aware of what was happening until it was too late. Some later claimed to have their suspicions of Kerviel, but if so they did not act on them. He was allowed to operate unmolested for some time, long enough to create record losses,[1] leading to organizational failure.

September 15, 2008. Lehman Brothers, one of the oldest banks on Wall Street, petitioned for bankruptcy. The shockwaves went around the world, rocking the global financial system and raising the spectre of recession. Tens of thousands of jobs were lost, tens of billions of dollars were wiped off the balance sheets not just of banks but of many other businesses.

To many, including many inside the financial system, this was a shocking event, simply incomprehensible. How had this old and respected institution got itself into this position? How could a bank like Lehman go from a seemingly solid position to bankruptcy in so short a time? In fact, as the subsequent two-year inquiry into the bankruptcy made clear, few at Lehman Brothers had any real understanding of the scale of the disaster threatening the bank until it was almost upon them. The *Financial Times*, commenting on the official report, noted that the bank lacked operational controls and took too many shortcuts, all of which put the bank itself at risk. No one, not even Dick Fuld, the bank's boss, seemed to have any real idea of what the bank's actual financial position was or where it stood. 'Lehman Brothers took excessive risks and betrayed all principles of financial good sense', says Peter Chapman in his history of the bank, *The Last of the Imperious Rich*.[2]

From the outside these sort of events appear incomprehensible. Yet they are numerous and frequent. These two examples come from the banking area, but there are plenty of non-banking examples too, as we will see in a moment. Public sector organizations too experience their extreme failures. And yet, all these organizations have controls, accounts, audits, which are intended to prevent such incidents. On the whole, these systems do work, and those who commit fraud or transgress in other ways are nearly always caught. But in cases like Barings, Société Générale and Lehman Brothers they are not caught soon enough. By the time the losses are discovered and those responsible for the failure are identified, the damage has been done. The critical question is, why does this happen?

The reason is deceptively simple. Research for this book, focusing on the linkages between business strategy, organizational structure and performance effects, shows that although most firms routinely gather and analyse huge amounts of data, too often the relevant and right data do not reach the right individuals. In addition, firms often have very fragmented and isolated data-gathering approaches that lack interconnectivity and a unified managerial language. More often than not, effective feedback loops that allow real-time adjustments without disrupting the overall organization are also not in place. Organizations also have huge problems in reconciling often opposing initiatives that stem from different divisions or business units and are not harmonized with each other. The result is a lack of a 'big picture' overview which creates a tactical instead of a strategic approach to management.

Our investigation also showed that the warning signs of crisis are nearly always there in advance of the crisis. But these signs are ignored or discounted by executives too busy and too distracted by tactical management and short-term trouble shooting. Top management needs systems in place to help executives understand what is going on everywhere in the organization *now*, not what went on last week or last quarter or last year. If those systems are not in place, or are in place but not working, then the organization itself is at risk.

Analysis of the examples cited above and other major failures suggests that some of the senior executives in these firms were hiding their heads in the sand. But it also appears that there was a lack of control, consistent control across the organization. To some extent, Lehman's senior managers for example were guessing in the dark – about the financial health of their own institution. And they were guilty too of what consultant and academic Tom FitzGerald calls 'looking in the rear view mirror'.[3] Their accounting and reporting frameworks were heavily geared towards past performance. They had no systems in place to help them understand the future and plot a course through it. Lacking an integrated framework that helps the organization to navigate through unexpected external events, they made bad decisions – like the decision to invest in toxic mortgage bonds. The result was the end of one institution, and severe damage to many others.

Now let us move fast forward to 20 April 2010. A massive explosion aboard the oil-drilling platform *Deepwater Horizon* killed eleven members of her crew and started a fire that could not be extinguished. Two days later the rig sank, leaving an uncapped oil well gushing crude oil into the Gulf of Mexico. The well was not finally capped until September 2010, four months later. By this time hundreds of thousands of gallons of oil had been spilled into the sea.

Owned by Transocean Ltd, a drilling contractor, the platform had been leased to BP and was operated by the giant oil company. BP was blamed for the accident. Anticipating huge costs for cleaning up the spill and subsequent litigation, the markets sent BP's shares into freefall. Its market value declined by £12 billion in the first ten days alone. At the same time a media storm broke over the corporation. In the American press in particular, BP and its executives were accused of reckless behaviour, of breaches of safety procedures and of callousness towards the inhabitants of the Gulf Coast affected by the spill. It did not matter that these accusations were exaggerated, and that the safety record on *Deepwater Horizon* up to this point had been very good. Nor did it matter that, as subsequent enquiries showed, companies other than BP bore a share of responsibility. Regardless of rights or wrongs, the damage done to BP's financial position, its reputation and its brand has been immense. A long road to recovery lies ahead.

In retrospect, the disaster itself is less important than BP's response to it. There was a strong perception that BP had been slow in its response, both in terms of moving resources into place to deal with the problem itself, and critically, in terms of protecting its public image. That *perceived* hesitation has cost the company billions, and even more severely, damaged nature and local communities almost irreparably.

What could have been done differently? Every part of an organization has a role to play in minimizing risks or in overcoming crises. This can only be achieved if a comprehensive, integrated, transparent, and dynamic management framework exists that is geared toward execution excellence.

Top management has to have clear, deep-reaching information tools and decision-making levers at its disposal, which it can pull in order to bring resources and people to bear on the problem. Those were lacking at BP. Since the crisis, BP has moved to a much tighter system with more information flowing to and from corporate headquarters and more effectively connecting the parts of the company. This should lead to a much faster and more effective response should a similar crisis occur. But as far as *Deepwater Horizon* is concerned, it is too late. The stable door is now securely shut, but the horse has long since bolted.

The complex world

> The economy is a marvel of complexity. Yet no one designed it and no one runs it. There are, of course, CEOs, government officials, international organizations, investors, and others who attempt to manage their particular patch of it, but when one steps back and looks at the entirety of the $36.5 trillion global economy, it is clear that no one is really in charge.[4]
>
> *Eric D. Beinhocker, The Origin of Wealth*

The examples cited above are by no means unique. Open any business newspaper on any given day and one will see many other examples of how the complexity of the business environment that Beinhocker refers to creates problems for management, from macro-level geopolitical issues that threaten economic stability to micro-level managerial issues that can nonetheless knock even the most robust strategy off track. Here are some examples of stories from the *Financial Times* of 25 October 2010:

> Toyota, the once shining company, continue to be tarnished by ongoing problems . . . Still on alert a year after the crisis.

Famous for its quality and for being a world-leading company, Toyota continues to suffer the fallout from its well-publicized problems in 2009.[5]

> Lego: for 70 years Lego experienced steady growth. But in 1998 the company started losing money. By 2003 sales had dropped by 20% . . . these two years represented the biggest losses in Lego history. The challenge: the company's focus on creativity, innovation and superior quality had created high complexity. The company had a

total of 12,500 stock-keeping units, with more than 100 different colours and more than 11,000 suppliers etc. Fixing: new vision . . . a new strategy . . . a new model. Results: sales up . . . customer satisfaction up . . . the unexpected problem . . . a lot of things did not work as expected . . . Key lessons: complexity in terms of a company offering too many products creates very high costs . . . The idea of exceeding customer requirements might lead to an overly complex and costly value chain . . . These strategic relations must be proactively managed in a structured and planned way.

The Truth about Ikea [book review]. The book sets out to demolish the idealized image of Ikea . . . issues about succession might negatively impact Ikea's future . . .

SAP has been ordered to pay $1.3 billion in damages to arch-foe Oracle, for software stolen by a subsidiary company it acquired for $10 million in 2005.

Bank of Ireland: The bank can not stand anymore on its own.

UBS: Sued by Madoff trustee for $2 billion.

Thus on just one day, one newspaper's news shows examples of well-intentioned executives managing companies as best they can, coping with a wide range of complexities, problems and unexpected issues but still failing to execute business strategies effectively. We ask: was reality more complex than these CEOs and their boards had foreseen, or were they just simply assuming that based on a clear mission and a good vision, they could execute a long-lasting strategy? Books like *Built to Last* and *Good to Great* tend to encourage managers to believe this to be so but we have our doubts.[6]

Over the past few years we have seen billions wiped off the balance sheets of companies around the world. Once respected corporate names have fallen prey to forces that, on the surface at least, seem to be beyond their control. Whenever things like this happen, we look for answers; but we never seem to find any, or at best we only seem to find answers 'with the benefit of hindsight'. Were the heads of our large institutions simply asleep at the wheel? Or is it that these institutions have become so large and so complex that 'no one is really in charge'?[7] Our large corporations operate across vast distances, and employ tens of thousands or even hundreds of thousands of people from many different cultures and backgrounds. They offer wide ranges of products and services to many diverse customer segments. Never mind the issue of too big to fail: are our institutions now 'too big and/or too complex to manage', or at least, too big and/or too complex to be manageable?

What could have prevented these once shining examples of companies cited above from running into trouble? Is there any way that these problems could have been avoided? Is the world simply too complex to be understood and managed? Do we indeed have the required brainpower and the capability to understand all the dynamics around us, today and tomorrow, with the acceleration of globalization, constantly changing settings, with so little clarity or visibility; or is there a better way to help reduce complexities and increase visibility?

Certainly managers, prominent consulting firms like McKinsey or the Boston Consulting Group, and leading management scholars are trying. New management ideas emerge seemingly every day. These new ideas undoubtedly often add value, but they also often add complexity. In their recent article in the *Harvard Business Review*, David J. Snowden and Mary E. Boone stated that complexities in organizations arise because of a proliferation of large numbers of interacting yet divergent elements.[8] These new elements often do not arise in a linear fashion. In reality, even minor changes can produce disproportionately major consequences for the organization. Since the environment in which we work is dynamic and relatively unpredictable, pre-designed and standard responses or solutions are often not effective. Nor can we expect too much from more centralized approaches and attempts to establish more 'control'.

As noted above, the solution is better 'management of management'. In other words, we need to apply the same rigorous, analytical ideas that we apply to finance, marketing and production, to management itself. Concepts like continuous improvement and constant adaptability in the face of change need to be applied to the management of businesses, not just their operations.

The days of excessive trust in rigid strategic thinking and robust analysis and planning are gone. Flexibility and swift strategic reactions are the keys to survival. As the English philosopher, biologist and sociologist Herbert Spencer observed long ago, it is not the strongest or the smartest species that survive, but those best capable of adaptation.[9] This might suggest the need for localized solutions capable of greater adaptation; even companies operating globally must focus on the local environment too. There is merit to this idea, but these localized solutions need to be designed in such a way that they are easily integrated in the larger system without increasing complexities.

BOX 1.1 TOO BIG TO REGULATE?

But what if the need to impose appropriate regulation itself becomes a limit on the allowable size or complexity of firms? In short, can a firm be too big to regulate?

In any such discussion it is important first to distinguish between several dimensions of big. The first dimension is the multiplicity of products and markets in which a company is involved. In context, this means companies that operate in commercial and investment banking, trading, insurance, and dozens of other product lines that are all 'financial', but which have different attributes, externalities, and regulatory requirements. Call this 'firm complexity'.

'Organizational complexity', the second dimension, tends to follow firm complexity, but it isn't the same. This dimension has to do with the number and diversity of business structures owned by a single parent company. The larger and more varied the number of corporate entities owned or controlled by a single parent, the more layers of vertical ownership; and the more complex the cross-ownership claims, the more complicated the structure.

The third and final dimension is 'structural bigness'. This is about having a large market share in a well-defined product and geographic market. This is the traditional meaning of big in the industrial organization field of economics. It is bigness within a market, or market dominance.

For most financial (as well as non-financial) products, structural bigness is policed by competition (antitrust) laws. (The insurance industry has enjoyed an antitrust exemption that Congress is now reconsidering.) Because I assume these laws will continue to be enforced, I assume structural bigness is not a factor in making a firm too big to regulate.

For the other two dimensions of bigness, product and organizational complexity, it's a different story. In a nutshell, when the range of one firm's market and organizational activities grows too large, it often becomes politically or administratively impossible to do a good job regulating it, whatever the particular tools and processes regulators use.

Firm complexity challenges regulation because it requires regulatory agencies with enormous resources to understand the linkages between extremely different financial product markets. To regulate a firm engaged in insurance, banking, investment banking, trading, and other products, a single regulatory agency will have to possess an unbelievably broad range of skills, tools, and resources. This is not to deny that there is a careful balance to be struck between too much and too little regulatory overlap, acknowledging sometimes-conflicting problems such as regulatory capture and forum shopping.

For purely practical reasons, organizational complexity also makes regulation ineffective. As businesses get successively more complex and varied business structures, the ability of regulatory agencies to understand the company's financial position simply fades away. Remember the well-documented infamous Enron example. Enron built a financial structure so complex that regulators could never understand what it was up to, even following its downfall. When the investigative staff of the U.S. Federal Energy Regulatory Commission (FERC) was directed to look into the company's electricity trading practices, the complexity of the issues confronting staff and the agencies cooperating with the Commission was such that too much time would have been required to fully understand Enron's and other market participants' activities in the energy markets. For example, the FERC spent a considerable amount of time analysing Enron's massive information technology (IT) systems that were used to harness information to Enron's advantage. In short, the IT systems were functionally equivalent to the IT systems of a national trading exchange, e.g., a stock exchange, coupled with the credit and risk systems of a large national bank, and linked to a large telecom company. Because Enron traded 1,700 different products on-line around the world, the trading had to be linked together in a secure manner. However, the system was so complex that nobody really understood which [aspects] of the risk were critical and which ones were not. Fortunately for the FERC, its objectives in the investigations were confined to Enron's role in the Western power crisis of 2000–2001. No full accounting of Enron's overall actions was sought, and none has been produced until today.[10]

(Peter Fox-Penner, a leading expert on regulation
at The Brattle Group)

Another writer on complexity, Kurt Richardson, has pointed out that we need to make distinctions between things which are *complex* and those which are merely *complicated*.[11] Complex systems are complex by necessity; they evolve to meet external pressures and the needs of those who use them. A coral reef is a highly complex structure, but all of its parts are essential to the survival of the coral itself and the fish, plants and other organisms that inhabit it; alter one element, and you threaten the balance of the entire system. Complicated systems, on the other hand, are ones which have evolved by chance rather than necessity. Some of their functions may be duplicated, others may be obsolete. We can think of government civil services with their large shambling bureaucracies full of duplication and waste, as an example.

But even when it comes about as a result of positive forces, such as innovation and growth, complexity can threaten to take over our lives. How many chairmen and CEOs of large organizations know what is going on, every minute of every day, throughout their organizations? None, because it is impossible for one individual to know and understand these large and complex organizations in their entirety. As one of our colleagues says, 'having a bigger haystack means it is harder to find the needles'. Therefore, top leadership has to trust to some extent that the organization is proceeding towards its strategic goals and nothing serious is going wrong behind the scenes. Because of the increasingly complex challenges companies face, the management of management, the management of the total managerial process with a focus on aligned but flexible organizational decision-making, has become the key task of leaders today.

Scale and scope mean that business organizations of today are very different from the business organizations of a hundred years ago or fifty years ago, or even twenty years ago. And it is not just big organizations that are affected. Today, even small businesses connected to the Internet can manage a complex network of value chain partners or diverse customer groups around the world. Software firms often operate in this way, but they are not the only ones. Firms in fields such as speciality food production, fashion design and boutique travel agencies routinely operate in international markets and have to deal with all the added complexity that immediately builds up once they step outside their home markets.

The problem, or one of them, is that we are still trying to manage these complex organizations using the management methods of twenty, fifty or a hundred years ago. For example, look at how most organizations today – even comparatively small ones – are compartmentalized and divided into

departments, divisions, strategic business units. This kind of divisionaliza-
tion was invented a hundred years ago by Pierre du Pont and Alfred P.
Sloan, and employed with great effect at General Motors. A sprawling,
uncoordinated, decentralized organization was given structure and focus,
which enabled it to overtake Ford as the world's leading automobile maker.
It was, as Alfred Chandler argued in *The Visible Hand*, the right business
model for the time.[12]

But is it still the right business model? Are big companies really benefit-
ting from economies of scale? If so, why are they not bigger than they
already are? Why does 90 per cent of the global workforce still work for
small and medium-sized businesses? And if size really does result in synergy
and efficiency, why are so many large companies priced on the stock
market at a 'conglomerate discount' and not at a premium? Why do so
many companies, after growing, then find that they have to scale down and
become 'small' again in order to become efficient and effective? The
answer, as we shall see, is that these companies are not being effectively
managed. Companies have effective and well-engineered systems that
enable them to manage all sorts of processes and tasks – except for management itself.

Building the case for change

Today, very many businesses are still organized following Chandler's
structural model. While the value of structure is undeniable, a rigid system
often turns divisions, departments or individual business unit into silos.
These silos operate in so self-contained a manner that little information
leaks out of or into them. They are cut off from the rest of the organization. When functional silos are working at cross-purposes, it is time for
somebody to 'take charge', argues Jagdish Sheth in his book *The Self-
Destructive Habits of Good Companies*.[13]

Today, top management needs strategic and operational control, perhaps
more than ever, but not at the cost of crippling the organization's ability to
adapt to internal or external challenges. The philosopher of organizational
behaviour Charles Handy, in *The Empty Raincoat*, speculated on the relationship between complexity and chaos, and whether perhaps chaos is the
natural order of things.[14] Others criticize modern management, implicitly
at least, for being too linear and analytical, for focusing too much on trying
to attack problems head on and solve them directly.[15] In his book *Obliquity*,
John Kay wrote that

great cathedrals are built by an oblique process. The builders lived in a world in which the evolution of objectives, states and actions was mutually supportive: a world influenced by unpredictable consequences of interaction with other people and organizations; a world whose unpredictable complexity defied precise analysis or calculation; a world suffused with uncertainty in which the specification of problems was inevitably incomplete.[16]

Kay goes on to say that 'in an imperfectly understood world, high-level objectives are best achieved by constantly balancing their incompatibilities, through obliquity'. But thinking obliquely, or thinking around problem and opportunities, does not mean thinking intuitively or irrationally. On the contrary, says Kay, 'rationality is defined as consistency, and consistency is formally equivalent to maximization'.[17] Rational thinking and consistent systems make for both greater efficiency and greater effectiveness. We know how important rationality is; without it, many things would not work. Ships and aircraft plot courses by measuring and calculating distances. If they do not, then the ship is likely to run aground or the aircraft will run out of fuel and crash. Architects and engineers design and build houses by measuring space, calculating angles, working out where pipes and ducts must run, determining the stress that load-bearing walls will need to bear, and so on. They also specify the task of the plumber, the carpenter, the electrician and other tradesmen, all to the smallest detail, all in a well-aligned, consistent, complete and comprehensive way. If architects fail to do this, then the building will be inefficient, fragile and possibly dangerous.

Management in today's increasingly complex business environment requires *more* and better management, not less. In order to understand what is going on in the 'world' and in their own organizations, managers need pertinent information and the ability to reach all parts of the firm. Management frameworks can help to reduce complexity, or at least, make it more manageable. The purpose of this book is to help managers to understand frameworks and why and how they can help.

From new frames of mind to new frames of management

In order to cope with the growing complexities of organizations we need to find a new way of thinking about management itself. Too many managers are stuck in the 'silo' mentality to the point where often they are no longer able to recognize the larger organizational picture. During our research and many hours of executive education teaching, we have found that most managers utilize management tools only in a limited way. Indeed, incentive and reward structures often *encourage* people to think one-dimensionally, with a focus on the 'numbers'. Many do not look outside of their own boxes, at least not often enough.[18] All too often, managers are only rewarded for achieving individuals' targets or at best for group targets that they cannot influence individually anyway. This encourages a straight-ahead focus on personal goals without thinking about the larger system and the implications of one's own work on that system. Sometimes companies will have a small percentage of incentives linked to synergetic behaviour, but this is never enough to encourage people to think and act multi-functionally and across a broad spectrum.

A new and better frame of mind and approach is required in order to help people moving from:

small view to big *vision*
one-sided to multi-dimensional *thinking*
tactical to strategic *managing*
single to cooperative *acting.*

This is easy to say, and we recognize that such a shift will be challenging to implement. One of the first prerequisites is leadership. Leaders need to create the conditions that will allow, support and enable managers to think outside their own boxes while looking at their organizations and the world as a whole in more holistic way. Further, incentive systems should be designed in such a way that they support these boundary-spanning behaviours.[19] And finally, as we will argue later in this book, leaders should create the organizational capabilities and settings that will enable people to operate with different *frames of minds*, supported by strongly improved *frames of management processes.*

The complexity context

When we think about complexity, most of us think about external complexities, for instance those coming from increasing and changing market conditions, regulations or external bureaucracies. In fact, most of these are beyond the power of managers to change.

Complexities within organizations are often overlooked. This is ironic, because these are often complexities that managers and leaders *do* have the power to change (see Figure 1.1).

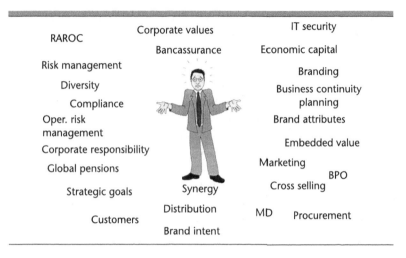

RAROC
Corporate values
IT security

Bancassurance
Economic capital

Risk management

Diversity
Branding

Compliance
Business continuity
planning

Oper. risk
management
Brand attributes

Corporate responsibility
Embedded value

Global pensions
Marketing
BPO

Strategic goals
Synergy
Cross selling

Distribution
MD
Procurement

Customers

Brand intent

FIGURE 1.1 More and more issues haunt the manager

Companies need to look at themselves and ask some tough questions. Which complexities have been internally generated? What actions by management are creating additional complexities? What could management do to reduce these? Can the status of complexities within an organization be measured, for instance through a corporate complexity quotient or index? Of course, such measurement could itself become a source of complexities as well as adding a further layer of bureaucracy.

A satellite view of why the complex world is here to stay

The following 'big picture' observations might help to increase our understanding of why society is coping with growing complexities and why the world is becoming less predictable and less stable than it used to be.

1. Complexities expand faster than our capability to deal with complexities.
2. The Unknown Unknowns are much bigger than the (Un)Known Knowns.
3. Human behaviour is much underestimated by planners/decision-makers, who persist in believing that the world is rational.

As observed above, the growing need for flexibility – and need to reduce the rigidity that we have built into structures – paired with the threat of businesses becoming too complex to manage requires us to rethink our approach to organization. We need to see our large institutions not as large ocean liners, and more as a fleet of small boats that can steer more easily around cliffs and obstacles but that still stay together to help and support each other in rough waters (see Figures 1.2–1.4).

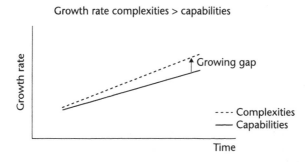

FIGURE 1.2 Complexities and capabilities

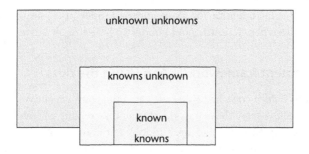

FIGURE 1.3 Too many unknowns

Note: The area of Known Knowns is very small as compared to the area of Knowns Unknown, which we typically assume in our planning and decision-making after applying a certain probability factor. For instance, we know from experience that x per cent of drivers will have a car accident, but we don't know which drivers, where and when. Yet if the numbers are big enough these risks can be measured, priced for and be covered by (re-)insurance. The biggest area is however the Unknown Unknown space, where we are constantly moving into, without having planned for; not because our planning was insufficient, but just because the things that will or did happen are really unknown; for example, whether EU governments might default on their debts, or whether a tsunami will suddenly strike a nuclear power station.

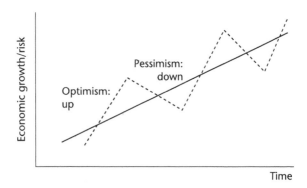

FIGURE 1.4 Human behaviour causing ongoing cycles

Note: Economic cycles have been and will always be there. As economists have known for more than century, it is in our genetic make-up as people (including consumers, government and business leaders/managers, even regulators) to exaggerate on the 'up side' as well as on the 'down side'. This causes ongoing crises and cycles, thus making straight-line growth nearly impossible.[20]

Let us look at how to reduce these growing complexities within organizations by the introduction of management frameworks, similar to what architects do when designing and building a house or an office building.

Management frameworks: connecting the dots

In order to reduce complexity and increase efficiency, executives can learn a variety of lessons from the real world. Rather than relying entirely on abstract theories of organization, they need to look at the world of concrete things. Let us return again to the example of the architecture of a building, or perhaps the design of a particularly good website. Things and options are generally well-listed, ordered and in a complete, consistent and comprehensive way. Most things are well connected by applying frameworks, templates and lists or menus of options, guiding people (staff and customers) efficiently through the process of what they want to get done. On the shop floor and at the customer interface, we are actually quite good at designing processes organizations. But in the 'white collar' part of management, however, many people feel they are walking in a 'forest with too many trees'. It is easy to get lost because there are no road maps to show us where we are and how to best move forward. That is why we need management frameworks.

Management frameworks enable managers to harmonize planning, execution and organizational structure in a way that helps the organization to achieve its goals. There are many different types of management framework, and most managers probably have some experience of using one. Most are quite specialized in nature and relate to particular functions such as IT, process management or strategy. Others attempt to embrace the whole organization and help managers to run their businesses in a more holistic fashion. Some are high-end, top-management oriented and are intended to be used by very senior executives in large organizations. Others can be used by any organization, large or small, or by business units and teams within larger organizations.

Most organizations use frameworks as a matter of course. In fact, within any large organization it is likely that a number of specialist frameworks of the type mentioned above will already be partly in use. The problem with these is that they do not connect with each other, at least not very well. They were designed by specialists and are often used by specialists who, in effect, speak different languages. In organizations spread over a wide geographical area, we might find that some regions use one kind of framework while others use another kind. Cultural differences, within and outside the organization, might mean that reporting is done in very different and often incompatible ways.

We argue that while these frameworks as applied by specialized functional departments and (global or local) business units have their uses, they are not the whole answer. Organizations also need a single overarching management framework that encompasses the whole organization and its environment. To return once again to the comparison with architecture, the construction of a large building might require the completion of a whole set of specialist blueprints and drawings dealing with different aspects of the project. But there is always one master plan, within which these more specialist plans are subsumed. In an organization, there needs to be one master framework which spans the whole organization and governs the operations of all its parts without losing flexibility.

Any company can have such a management framework; indeed, we would argue that *every* company *should* have such a management framework! Without the guidance of an overall framework, there is a tendency to do things in an ad hoc manner, to react to events rather than driving forward, to act tactically instead of strategically. Frameworks provide direction and structure. They list and connect all the parts of the organization. They make visible what would otherwise be invisible. Thus they enable us to reach our objectives with more certainty, more precision, and less effort. In the end, frameworks help to reduce complexities and increase efficiencies in managerial thinking and acting.

Outline of this book

The purpose of this book is to look at overarching management frameworks which unify and connect all the parts of the organization, and to help readers understand how frameworks work and how to develop and apply them. In Chapter 2, we look at what management frameworks actually are, how they work and what kind of limitations they face. We also summarize and compare some of the most popular existing management frameworks and suggest how frameworks can be used to coach and guide existing and future executives and individuals in supervisory positions (auditors, board members, regulators, etc.) in how to achieve more effective *management of management*.

Chapter 3 sets out the key design questions for the development of a management framework. These include: What is the purpose of the framework? What is its scope? Who will drive the process? How do we incorporate widespread elements and individual goals and objectives? How will the framework be implemented and who will be responsible? How will the feedback loops work so as to lead to continuous improvement? How will the framework be adapted over time to capture new insights and realities on a day-to-day basis? What is needed to connect the framework with planning, knowledge management, pay-for-performance programmes as well as with the control and audit functions? After reading this chapter it should be obvious that the process of designing a management framework is closely connected with strategy formulation and implementation.

Chapter 4 picks up more closely on some of these concepts and looks at what we call *portfolio* drivers, based on the organization's vision, mission and strategic direction. We will look at how frameworks need to include portfolio options such as organic growth, acquisitions, partnerships, fixing or exiting business units, adding new countries or business lines, and so on. We will then show how these are to be linked to the overarching set of frameworks. For example, at GE overall performance is driven in part by buying, fixing, selling and exiting business lines and business units.

Chapter 5 follows on from this to look at *marketing* drivers: what the organization's products and services are, its channels of delivery, its customers and relationships with them. It will highlight the strong interdependencies between customers, products and channels, and then show how the overall management framework links to and supports the marketing effort.

Think of Citibank Corporate Banking, which will have special products such as M&A or IPOs for certain industry groups with a different distribution channel than the Citibank Retail Banking, which offers wealth management advice to retail customers. In other words, different customers require different products and different channels.

Chapter 6 looks at *organizational* drivers, in particular the often discussed question of aligning the organizational structure with strategy and execution, or in simple terms, who will do what and when. Here we look at defining the organizational setting (the organization chart), the differences between hierarchical and functional roles and reporting responsibilities, management development, incentives, performance culture and defining the role and task of the leader. This is, we freely admit, a rather more formal (but also more hands-on and pragmatic) view of organizations and communications than is in vogue at the moment. But organizational systems require at least a degree of clarity, structure and harmonization if they are to be effective, and a good management framework should aim to help provide that harmonization and clarity about responsibility. For example, when we look at a global company like Procter & Gamble, we need to ask: Who is in charge of the business in each country? The overall country manager, or the business line manager at headquarters? Who is responsible for functions such as risk and product development?

Chapter 7 moves on to discuss *operational* drivers, looking at issues such as aligning operational processes with functions like marketing, finance, in-country operations, sourcing and so on. How do these fit into the overall strategy? This chapter also discusses the links between strategic goals, assessing process effectiveness and efficiency, assessing operational risk, assessing IT capability and needs, and more generally linking the framework to all operations to improve customer satisfaction. We will discuss in more detail what we mean by 'efficiency' and 'effectiveness', and why we treat them as separate concepts. It will be seen too that this aspect of the framework in particular places a premium on flexibility and adaptability. The framework has to be able to support and accommodate necessary changes in operations to deal with changing markets, economic climates, good corporate responsibility and so on. As an example, we can think of Zara, the clothing retailer. Zara's fast response time when a new trend or 'fad' is identified, and its ability to go from design to production to market in the shortest time and at the lowest price possible, are crucial competitive advantages.

Chapter 8 looks at *reputational* drivers, an issue which in our view is far too seldom discussed in the literature on frameworks, or even on strategy more generally. Most organizations have only recently added this issue to their planning processes, and there is still a long way to go before it is really embedded in the implementation processes. Here we look at issues such as the organization's values, its level of integrity and ethics, the way it communicates internally and externally, and the reputational risks it faces. Managing these opportunities and risks and linking them to the rest of the organization is a key part of the task of the framework. Think of Siemens, which many years ago felt that it could meet the request of intermediaries to pay them large fees for booking contracts without raising too many integrity and ethical questions. As it turned out, Siemens was wrong. Only after very costly and lengthy legal procedures, and huge damage to its reputation, did the company manage to get rid of these bad practices.

Chapter 9 considers the *financial* drivers, basically those issues which are 'driven' by the finance departments, such as management reporting, control, balance sheet management, risk management and so on. Remember fast-growing Enron, which in the end got caught out by its lack of solid financial controls.

Chapter 10 looks at the *overall performance*, based on the company's vision, mission and strategic direction (including SWOT, trends and competitive position). By specifying the main quantitative and qualitative results management is aiming at, and then working with the six drivers above, the company should be able to achieve performance excellence. Finally, in Chapter 11, 'Connecting the Dots', we bring all the pieces together and look at how the parts of a holistic management framework fit together into a unified model.

Management frameworks are not panaceas. Having a management framework will not enable a company to avoid or solve all of its problems. Nor are management frameworks a substitute for strategy. Leaders and managers still have to come up with the strategy, but a good overarching framework will help them do so in a more concrete, consistent and effective way. It will also help them to respond to unplanned events and crises like those noted at the outset of this chapter – and it can be taken for granted that such crises will occur.

Frameworks bring greater certainty. They help managers to gather and assimilate reliable knowledge, analyse it, and make better, faster and more accurate decisions. That alone can be a priceless source of competitive advantage.

2

THE ARCHITECTURE OF AN ORGANIZATION

Frame: a construction, constitution, established order, plan or system.
(Oxford English Dictionary)

Frameworks bring and hold things together. When we think of common frameworks in ordinary use, we might think of the skeleton of a body, or the walls and roof trusses of a house, or the chassis of a car, or the trunk and branches of a tree. They provide a unifying structure around which a number of other things can cohere, and thus can interact and function as a whole. Thus the skeleton supports the body's organs and the circulatory and nervous systems, all of which work together in order to support life. The walls and roof trusses of a house support the roof and the plumbing and electrical systems and so create space for living. The wheels, engine and other parts of a car, when attached to the chassis, enable motion.

The point is that these individual elements – the plumbing of a house, the wheels of a car – are *on their own* unable to function. They need the rest of the structural framework in order to do anything useful. It is this framework that connects and allows them to work together so that the whole system does what it is supposed to do.

Many of the frameworks we use in everyday life are very simple. Examples include the alphabetical ordering of names in a telephone directory, or supermarkets putting groups of products together in order for customers to see more easily what is on offer. At a slightly more sophisticated level, think of how IKEA coaches its customers with simple frames and designs (without text) to help them efficiently assemble components into pieces of furniture.

These examples refer to 'hard' physical structures, but we can see the same principles at work when we look at 'soft' subjects. Take a schematic diagram of a business organization. It typically consists of a number of different functional departments and business units. Though most people are aware that the finance department, marketing department, sales teams, production facilities, R&D teams and human resources department are functional departments, many are unsure whether a sales channel or a country unit is a business unit or a 'support' unit. The framework must help to produce that clarity.

The larger the enterprise, the more geographically and functionally diverse it might be, the wider its product and services range, then the more complex that same organization is. What is more, it is likely to continue to grow and create exponentially expanding levels of complexity. The same applies when we think along dimensions such as strategic planning, strategy execution and organization. These dimensions are all quite abstract and invisible, until we put them in a more systematic order. When we look, for example, at an organization chart, we see an assortment of parts. Each of these teams and departments appears to be positioned and perhaps to operate quite on its own. What stops them from pulling apart, rather than pulling together? Traditionally, top management has used targets and bonus-setting as incentives to get people to pull together, but when the interests of an individual or a team is different from the rest of the organization, then the opposite effect might occur. Teams can end up focused on their own roles and their own goals rather than the whole organization. This creates disconnecting, non-aligned behaviour and processes which will not necessarily be in the interest of the rest of the organization or its stakeholders. .

Some readers will remember the diagrams we had as children, in puzzle books and so forth. What we saw on the page was a random assemblage of dots. When we drew lines between the dots, however, a picture emerged. Similarly, if you draw lines between the different parts of the business, we see a picture too: a picture that shows us how the organization reports, transmits information and is controlled. We call the process of linking all the elements of the business 'connecting all the dots', because the process is much the same; a group of apparently disconnected elements is transformed into a single unified – albeit diverse – enterprise. The dots themselves refer to strategy, execution and organization, and also to more specific issues such as risk management, customer services, branding and so on. The lines that connect all the dots represent the management frameworks that enable us to 'unify diversity'.

The 3Cs

The design of any framework, and the ordering of the components within that framework, must meet three criteria. They must be

1.   Consistent (that is, they are aligned with all strategic priorities)
2.   Complete (that is, all relevant drivers are listed)
3.   Comprehensive (all relevant specifics are available).

Only when this has been achieved will the management framework be effective and become an enabler. If not, then the framework will add complexities and reduce efficiency. Through the book we will emphasize and keep referring to these three criteria, the '3Cs'.

As we noted in the previous chapter, many businesses use sub-frameworks of different kinds. Individual departments or functions may have their own frameworks which pull together information in a way useful for that department or function. The most clear examples are the spreadsheets or frameworks/templates developed by the finance department, which should be used by all business units and functions when reporting their results. These are usually mandatory and standard frameworks, the purpose of which is to ensure that each reporting unit knows when, how and what to report; the content (the numbers) are unit specific. They also help the CFO to see all the numbers at once, presented in the same format so that easy comparisons can be made across the organization.

Interestingly, though, most other departments (like Operations or HR) and business units do not apply standardized frameworks/templates when communicating with their internal stakeholders. Instead, most functions or business units use their own reporting methods which take different forms and shapes. They are designed in isolation and to suit the needs of that particular department, without checking whether these templates are compatible with those of the other departments and business units. Only rarely do managers stop to check whether these templates are consistent, complete and comprehensive from a total organizational view. This is certainly not helpful if one wants to see more alignment in the entire organization, whether between the various vertical and/or horizontal layers in the organization or when discussing strategy, strategic priorities and implementation.

Particular geographic areas might also adopt frameworks/templates to suit their own needs. But these country-based frameworks frequently do not embrace the whole business, i.e. they don't connect well with the hundreds of other dots that make up other parts of the organization. And if they are allowed to proliferate – and they often do – situations develop where these frameworks begin to grind together. If they are not compatible – and they often are not – then the contradictions between them create friction which can interfere with efficiency of the business.

In the previous chapter we argued the need for a *single overarching management framework* which brings unity to the whole organization and ensures that all departments and business units work harmoniously together. What would such an overarching management framework look like? First, its purpose should be to align the company's strategy, execution and organization, and thus it needs to cover the entire organization: from head office to local business units and across all functions. But it should also connect the hundreds of dots that represent the organization's goals and activities. Thus it should include not only the big, high-level aspects of running an organization (like customer centricity or operational excellence) but it also should capture the smaller details which can suddenly become very important. To take just one example, IT security will become crucially important when a company's client list is being hacked.

The appearance of frameworks

> On all hands I found guess-work and muddling . . . A mass of incorrect operations was standardized into a routine. Stokers did not know how to stoke. Factory workers did not know how to operate their machines. Foremen did not know how to handle their men. Managing directors did not know . . . the principles of organization. Very few had *learned* how to do what they were doing.[1]
>
> *(Herbert Casson (management consultant, 1931)*

Frameworks are a fairly new concept in the 'soft' world, that is, in the management of the business and and other organizations (also referred to as the *white collar* part of the organization). From the Industrial Revolution onward, most of the improvements in management took place in manufacturing sectors and other related industries such as railways, and focused on

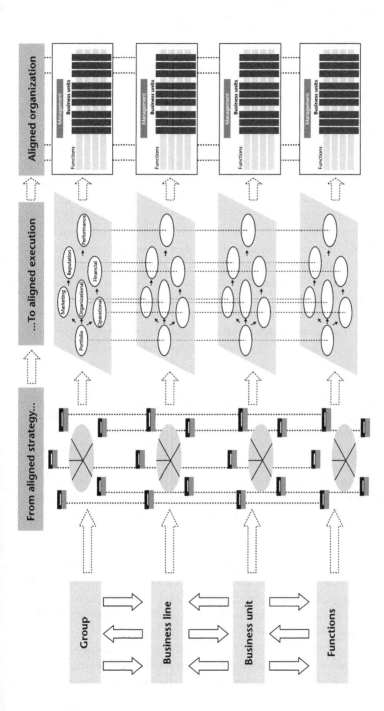

FIGURE 2.1 The overarching management framework

Source: The Towards Performance Excellence Management Framework.

'shop floor' or 'blue collar' efficiency. Investments in technology were followed by the development of more standardized work processes from the late nineteenth century onward. These showed how more could be produced with fewer resources, resulting in strong gains in productivity in the factory. Most of the wealth creation in the early twentieth century was due to these efficiency gains. Economies of scale were particularly sought after: the larger the scale (numbers of input and output) the higher the productivity and the lower the cost of production. This is still common today in industries such as consumer electronics which rely on mass production to keep unit costs down. In China we have seen how the benefits of scale in terms of China's fast growing economy have created hundreds of millions of new jobs. The use of standardized, well engineered and mapped (3Cs) processes were and still are key ingredients to these successes.

Yet this standardization of blue-collar work processes in the factory had not been accompanied by similar well engineered, 3Cs work and management processes elsewhere in the organization. Individual departments and business units can and do develop standardized business processes of their own. For instance the global HR department might set its goals and priorities for itself. Operational plans might not have been properly coordinated with marketing/sales. By definition, these bespoke processes — or frameworks — do not connect with other departments or business units. They are for internal use by that department or business unit only. They mostly cannot connect with other departments, and this gap in communications can actually create *dis*-economies of scale as the benefits of scale are lost. The question is, can we apply similar frameworks of better aligned 3Cs processes to 'white collar' management as the ones being used in 'blue collar' work processes?

Take for example Volkswagen, which produces many brands (VW, Audi, Skoda, Seat), with many products (small, mid-sized, sport, four-wheel drive) and in many countries (Germany, Spain, Slovakia, China, Brazil, etc.). There is thus a huge amount of diversity and complexity. Volkswagen attempts to resolve this by ensuring that most components, platforms, designs and productions processes are the same, or at least similar. This leads to optmization and efficiency so far as production is concerned. Economies of scale work, and it can be logically assumed that from a production point of view, the bigger the better.

But this logic does not always work when we come to the 'white collar' managerial aspects of the organization. Here, all of these different product ranges and geographies can create division and confusion. Thus another purpose of the general or set of overarching management frameworks is to create alignment and harmony and to provide a 'framework for frameworks' by ensuring that all the other frameworks and systems used are compatible. This will allow all the parts of the business to talk to the other parts in a context, language and numbers they can understand. Developing common systems for reporting and control right across the business, for example, enables managers everywhere – not just top management – to quickly understand and analyse data and information.

BOX 2.1 ARTIST'S ADVICE TO A CEO

An artist once famously wrote of his work: 'I want everybody and everything to be equally important; at the same time I want everybody and everything to be equally unimportant.' Managers would do well to listen to this advice.

Most managers add complexity by presenting their 'refreshing' and 'unique' strategic plans, without being consistent, complete and comprehensive; not only over time but also when discussing the same plan on different occasions. Furthermore they are inclined to focus on what they perceived to be the important priorities at the moment, without realizing that other 'drivers' could be equally important.

But would we do this on a production line, or in a design studio? When designing a new car, would be begin by setting the three most important strategic priorities as (1) wheels, (2) motor and (3) fuel tank? Should there not be discussion as well of the electronics, or the brakes? Instead, management should start with the notion that 'everything is equally important and equally unimportant'. The question becomes then, what is really important? The answer is the total process in designing a good car, or for the purpose of this book, the total process of leading and managing the entire organization in the most efficient and effective way! Focusing on just three strategic priorities might sound and feel good, but it will entirely misrepresent those issues, and overlook other issues that might matter. Think about how overlooking server operational continuity resulted in inconvenience for hundreds of millions of BlackBerry users and wiped billions of dollars off the value of RIM's stock.

Recent academic research from Thunderbird University questioned whether large MNCs are applying the principles of the 3Cs when communicating externally to their key stakeholders about their strategy, execution and organization. The data were taken from their annual reports, quarterly results reporting, investor presentations, etc. Put simply, the findings were that companies are not answering the 'what, how and who' questions that people are asking in a 3Cs way.[2] For example, most presentations made by companies to stakeholders were short of consistency in language and specifics (thus incomplete and incomprehensive, or even incomprehensible). One comment was, 'They are long on feel-good news, but short on real, factual news.' In one presentation the company explained its international strategy was to focus on 'Asian countries', while in another case the company stated that it will focus on 'emerging markets'. The context suggested that there was no change in these companies' overseas strategy, and it is safe to assume that they meant the same thing; but in fact the presentation was communicating totally different things, thus adding complexities and increasing the 'invisibility' to stakeholders. Though this research was based on 'auditable and legally robust' external reporting, one can assume that the internal way of communicating the company's strategy, execution and organization processes might be equally flawed and inconsistent.

Most managers underestimate the importance of consistent language. Even if the same words are being used, most people give different meanings to simple words as 'vision, mission and strategy'. Similarly, 'marketing' to some people means 'branding' while to others it is synonymous with 'sales'. By simply defining and embedding a consistent language in the total process through the management framework, leaders can help to reduce complexities and increase efficiency. At the same time they will make the invisible (more) visible!

A short history of efficiency improvement

The first management frameworks were developed, at least in part, as ways of countering the rampant inefficiencies that plagued most businesses. Large businesses in particular had become too complex to be run in an ad hoc manner. Increases in scale and scope meant that top managers were losing control. Management frameworks attempted to bring a more systematic approach to the art of running a business.

The two best-known early management frameworks were scientific management, developed in the USA, and the administrative framework described by the French mining engineer Henri Fayol. The latter framework was very simple. Fayol set out a series of seven managerial tasks, which was summarized by a later writer, Luther Gulick, in the acronym POSDCORB: planning, organizing, staffing, directing, co-ordinating, reporting and budgeting. This was a fairly crude and simplistic tool, but it did at least give managers an idea of what they should be doing. Scientific management took the opposite approach, starting at the bottom of the organization and defining tasks and roles and then setting optimum performance targets for individual workers, then creating aggregate performance targets for teams and business units, and finally for the organization as a whole.[3]

Starting from the 1960s there was a proliferation of strategic frameworks, notably those of Igor Ansoff and Michael Porter, the latter of which is still widely used.[4] Still in use too is the 4Ps framework developed by Philip Kotler, originally designed as a marketing tool but often used by companies as a total management framework.[5] Many of these frameworks were problematic and of limited scope, however, in that they focused on strategic intent and planning and neglected execution. Critics such as the Canadian management guru Henry Mintzberg argued that they did not reflect the reality of how businesses were run.[6] More recent strategic frameworks such as the Return on Strategy framework developed by Andersen *et al.* have adopted a more holistic approach and included execution elements as well.[7]

The 1990s and 2000s saw a proliferation of specialist frameworks in areas such as marketing (customer relationship management, for example), finance and operations, and enterprise resources planning. It also saw the beginning of a new approach to general management frameworks. The most notable of these was the Balanced Scorecard, developed by Robert Kaplan and David Norton, which has been widely used.[8] The Balanced Scorecard became popular because it was easy to implement and could be used by small teams, even individuals, in contrast to frameworks such as Scientific Management which were costly and time-consuming. Other general management frameworks have followed since.

Management frameworks today

As well as the Balanced Scorecard, several other management frameworks have been developed and are in more or less widespread use. In the late

1990s Pryor, White and Toombs developed the 5Ps model (purpose, principles, processes, people, and performance).[9] This was a fairly simple framework intended for small business. McKinsey's 7S framework was a more holistic framework aimed at organizational transformation.[10] Accenture's SAP framework is an enterprise resources processing-based combined framework that integrates an IT driven approach with management relationships.

There are many more concepts out there, and new generic approaches are emerging all of the time. Different managerial preferences will make different frameworks more appealing to leaders and managers. In order to illustrate this last point, let us take a brief look at some of the more popular frameworks.

McKinsey 7S model

The 7S management framework was first introduced by Tom Peters and Robert Waterman in their book *In Search of Excellence*.[11] The term '7S' refers to the seven elements within the framework: (1) strategy, (2) structure, (3) systems, (4) staff, (5) skills, (6) style, and (7) shared values. The framework simulates an interconnected molecule with one element, share values, at its centre and the six other elements forming an interlinked hexagon around it. The main premise of the framework is the interconnectedness of the seven elements, and it is emphasized that management needs to take all seven elements into account simultaneously rather then privileging any one over the others. The ultimate goal is internal organizational alignment.[12] The model can be applied to specific teams, departments, or for the organization as a whole. In particular it is useful for helping to integrate organizations during mergers and acquisitions.

'Strategy' and 'structure' are self-explanatory. 'Systems' here refers to organizational processes and routines, and 'style' refers to the leadership style of top management. 'Staff' is an umbrella term encompassing the overall quality of employees and their general capabilities, while 'skills' refers to their actual expert competencies. 'Shared values' refers to culture and the attitudes of management and staff. The central positioning of shared values shows, according to Peters and Waterman, that they are directly connected with the functioning of all the other elements.[13] Applying 7S requires a two-step approach. The first step is to map the actual configuration of the elements. The second step describes the intended ideal configuration. The gaps between the two can then be identified and analysed.[14]

The 7S framework has been criticized for being overly simplistic. The seven concepts themselves can appear divorced from the reality of what people do in their day-to-day jobs, like sales, risk management, product development, career development, building partnerships and so on. However the main shortfall of the 7S model is its lack of specific drivers or measurement categories. It can be difficult to identify the most critical sub-elements for each category. For example, when considering skills we know in detail what kinds of skills the organization possesses – or lacks – and where these are distributed. This high-level overview might overlook real weaknesses in some parts of the organization, and some important elements might not be aligned because, in fact, they were not considered in the first place. A detailed case study and very deep insights into the organization and its processes are crucial to make the 7S framework work. Another criticism is that the 7S framework does not include any connection with the external environment of the organization.

The 5Ps model

The 5Ps framework was developed by Mildred Golden Pryor, Chris White and Leslie Toombs as a tool for small business owners.[15] The first and most important of the five Ps was business *purpose*. The other four elements were (2) principles, (3) processes, (4) people and (5) performance.[16]

In the 5Ps framework, strategic purpose determines structure, which in turn is defined by principals and processes. Structure in turn shapes the behaviours of people with the intention of creating improved performance. Feedback loops connect all the elements with purpose and then help to guide improvement processes.[17] Metrics and measurements play an important role in tracking status. The authors of the 5Ps framework also discuss alignment, but are not specific as to how it should be achieved.

The 5Ps framework is considerably simpler than the McKinsey 7S framework thanks in part to its straightforward linear design. The 5Ps framework could be developed step by step and parts of the framework could be useful without the framework having to be adopted in its entirety. Implementing the five Ps framework would be less disruptive to daily business activities and demand fewer resources for implementation.

The Balanced Scorecard and strategy maps

The Balanced Scorecard was first introduced as a stand-alone concept in 1992 in a *Harvard Business Review* article by Robert Kaplan and David Norton.[18] The purpose of this approach was to provide a tool that measures performance beyond traditional, purely financial indicators. The Balanced Scorecard concept appealed to organizations that did not seek superior financial performance as their primary objective – for example, not-for-profit organizations – and also to strategists who adopted it for measuring those managerial activities that could not directly be assessed by reviewing financial balance sheets.[19]

The Balanced Scorecard does not ignore the financials, but instead adds three further dimensions to the strategic assessment planning processes: customers, organizational processes, and learning and growth. The aim is to measure both current performance and how well the organization is actually positioned for future performance.

According to Kaplan and Norton, the Balanced Scorecard provides three main advantages. First, it allows managers to identify the key focus areas that lead to superior results. Second, it supports the integration of organizational initiatives, including product or service quality, human resources activities, research and development, or other long-term activities. Third, it allows for breaking down the usually higher-order strategy objectives into finer grained measurable activities that can then be attributed to individual departments and managers. For example investment in training might not lead directly to higher profits but it may improve the skills of the customer service representatives, which will then lead to higher levels of customer loyalty, which should lead to higher returns.[20]

It should be pointed out that these measures are meant to complement financial performance data and do not replace them. In fact the authors argue that in combination with the (1) traditional financial measures, (2) customer scores, (3) learning and growth scores, and (4) internal business processes, scores further enable organizations to be more forward looking, which then leads to better risk and cost-benefit assessments.[21]

Business processes are the fourth dimension included in the Balance Scorecard. Business process scores measure the internal effectiveness of a business, or in other words, how well the business operates. There are two categories within this dimension: (1) mission-oriented processes including production processes and innovation effectiveness, and (2) support processes. Mission-oriented processes are typically more difficult to capture and measure, while support processes are easier to measure thanks to their more repetitive characteristics.[22]

One reason why the Balanced Scorecard has been so successful is that it integrates the four basic perspectives into one simple framework. Each of the four dimensions is further sub-divided into four categories: (1) objectives, (2) measures, (3) targets, and (4) initiatives. For example, if the objective was to expand sales across the product portfolio, the relevant measure would be the increase in the number of products sold. The target would be set accordingly and specific initiatives to reach the objectives would be defined as, for example, sales promotions that include the number of product bundles offered, etc. The business process category is particularly important here. If set up correctly, this measure can lead to the identification of errors within the system at specific points.

The Balanced Scorecard evolved from a simple assessment tool into a strategic management framework when the concept of strategy maps was added.[23] Strategy maps enable companies to visualize cause-and-effect relationships relating to the individual scorecards of different departments or business units. Strategy maps show how the different layers of an organization connect with each other and how they influence overall performance.

The most common failures relating to the Balanced Scorecard approach include too many or too few measures, ambiguity concerning the 'real' performance drivers, inappropriate weighting of the individual measures, a lack of annual reviews of the relevance of individual measures, and most importantly, poor organizational design and the lack of structural adjustment based on initial scorecard outcomes. Kaplan and Norton themselves identified a number of risks relating to the Balanced Scorecard, including insufficient top management commitment, too few individuals involved, implementation of the scorecard at the highest organizational level only, overly lengthy development and implementations processes, and inexperienced scorecard champions or consultants.[24]

Accenture's A-EPM

The Accenture Advanced Enterprise Performance Management Solution (A-EPM) is different from other management frameworks in that it is integrated with one the of the world's leading enterprise resources software solutions developed by the German-based IT giant SAP. A-EPM is intended to be a financial and commercial planning and analysis tool that supports organizations in managing all aspects of the business towards optimum performance.[25] It takes in a range of planning and management aspects, including business intelligence, overall data management, corporate governance, risk and compliance, budgeting, forecasting and general reporting.

The A-EPM framework rests on the foundation of the raw data provided by SAP, and adds a strategic management angle to the SAP solution. The goal is to allow firms to develop more advanced capabilities, achieve better insights, improve managerial decision-making and react more quickly to changing market conditions.[26] The framework is built around the concept of 'business enablers' that stand at the centre of a circular process. That process begins with the formulation of the business strategy, which then leads to the target-setting process, followed by the definition of operating parameters and the monitoring of the actual operations. This then loops back to the business strategy. The framework is intended to be comprehensive, incorporating key performance metrics and supporting tools.

The Accenture A-EPM framework is of course not without its critics. There have been complaints about inexperienced consultants trying to implement the framework who are either not familiar enough with the details of the complex SAP software, or who do not understand the businesses that they are working with.[27] In order to implement A-EPM the organization must also have a functioning SAP enterprise resource processing solution in place, or be about to establish one. The investment costs are substantial, and the framework can only be practical for organizations that have reached a certain size and are spread across business units and/or regions.

The TPE framework

In 2003, Jacques Kemp, then newly appointed chief executive officer (CEO) of ING Insurance/Asset Management Asia Pacific, faced the task of integrating and improving the overall efficiency of the fourteen local ING operations with ten regional functions. Dissatisfied by the standard solutions provided by some management consulting firms, he developed his own management framework that he later labelled Towards Performance Excellence (TPE).[28] Once the TPE frameworks had been rolled out and all business units and functions were using it in order to manage their diverse businesses, clear progress was seen in terms of greater efficiency, better audit reports, higher growth rates and higher satisfaction scores among staff and customers. Other ING units and other companies soon started to apply these frameworks, with similar results.

For Kemp the overarching issue was the optimization of what he called the 'management of management'. He argued that many executives would define their five top priorities as, for example, customer focus, superior operations, execution, market leadership and so on, but would not define these categories so that they would be well understood throughout the entire organization. He also felt that most priorities were rather arbitrarily chosen and not the result of a 3Cs analysis of what the strategic priorities indeed should be. Why would risk management, for instance, not be a priority? Appropriate 3Cs organizational structures that enabled well-aligned execution of business strategies by all relevant participants in the entire organization were also often lacking. He believed that executives have to provide management with the right tools to get the job done. The many invisible management issues should be made more visible to all participants.

Kemp compared this with the role of coaches when building professional sports teams. Coaches help the individual players to build personal skills and at the same time build organizational capabilities by adding structure and discipline, showing players how to position and 'move' as an entire team. Both the Dutch national soccer team and the famous Dutch club Ajax became highly successful when their coach Rinus Michels introduced the players to the concept of 'total football'. In other, less professional teams, each player plays for himself and sets his own wishes above the team's need to win. He argued that most managers in most organizations are not playing 'total football'.

Kemp went on to design a total process which *listed*, *ordered* and *specified* all the things that his company had decided were important and needed to be executed in order to be successful. The process was designed and implemented with the involvement of all managers across the entire organization. By giving all managers through the entire organization a complete, consistent and comprehensive set of tools, Kemp saw his key role as leader to coach his managers so that they would play 'total football', or in this case, 'total management', working not as individuals but as a cohesive team. As soon as the total management process, supported by the appropriate management frameworks and tools was rolled out, the *social and economic cohesion* between the operating parts of the business proved itself a very effective way to improve the overall financial *and* non-financial performance of the entire organization. This case was later documented in a business case study by the Richard Ivey School of Business at the University of Western Ontario.[29]

Benefits of management frameworks

Modern businesses, even fairly small ones, are highly complex. The speed of change, both internally and in the external environment, can be very rapid. Managers struggle to keep up with the pace of change, and to make decisions that are relevant and accurate.

The key task for managers when aiming to reduce complexities and increase efficiencies is to build frameworks and templates that incorporate all of those things or actions that an organization wants to get done, now and in the future. Let's call these 'drivers', since things or actions management wants or needs to get done are typically aimed at 'driving' performance. Truly dynamic frameworks, which will enable the organization to take its strategy forward, should:

1. list all of these drivers;
2. order these drivers into a logical set of priorities;
3. add short descriptions, objectives and KPIs, then cascade all these drivers down in good, logical order until there is nothing left on the *known* drivers and sub-drivers to be done;
4. update those (sub) drivers which the organization decides to add, delete or redefine/reset as the strategy is taken forward;
5. ensure that this process is applied company-wide and across all activities, including planning, auditing, agenda-meetings, communication, performance measurement and variable compensation schemes, internal and external reporting, and competition analysis.

If this can be done, then the benefits of a well-designed framework system are several. They include the following:

Better and more efficient planning. Once the frameworks and templates are designed and implemented, planning and reporting become a matter of updating what has changed rather than starting from scratch every time. There is also a positive certainty that all the key issues involved in planning have been considered and analysed.

Better and more efficient execution. Managers lose precious time when they plan and report in different, incomplete formats with inconsistent, uncomprehensive content. For instance, if managers report that their goal is to reduce costs and at the same time be more customer-focused, there could well be situations where these goals are opposed to one another. A framework which meets the 3Cs criteria will ensure that goals are properly aligned. This frees up management time for important issues like innovation or managing the unexpected and unknown issues that crop up almost on a daily basis. At ING Asia Pacific managers were coached to plan their agenda in such a way that 80 per cent of their time could be spent on the 'expected things' and the remaining 20 per cent would be devoted to unexpected problems and opportunities. In this way managers can become more effective and adaptive.

Better sharing of knowledge. Every business, every manager, needs knowledge in order to function. In their book on virtual organizations, Malcolm Warner and Morgen Witzel compared knowledge to the lifeblood of an organization.[30] It needs to be circulated, and to be constantly replenished. Without it, the organization quickly begins to wither. Knowledge enables managers to plan, make decisions, act and then monitor the consequences of those actions. One of the functions of a management framework is to circulate knowledge rapidly, so that people know what is going on around them (rather than only finding out too late, as so often happens).

Better operational and financial control and reporting. As well as knowing what is going on around them, managers also have to be capable of influencing events and making certain that their decisions get implemented. Management frameworks enable managers to exert control and to make sure that others are sticking to the script and all working together. They help to ensure that performance is consistent and is focused on goals by using well-designed quantitive *and* qualitative planning templates that are shared in common right across the organization. Companies that do not have the necessary management tools and frameworks will have to allocate huge resources to get the job done or risk becoming non-compliant. In this way it will be more likely that the incorrect positions and exposures reported by traders like Kerviel and Leeson will be spotted earlier on

Better decision-making. Better informed managers make better decisions. Management frameworks enable managers to tap the relevant sources of information and knowledge when they need to make a decision, then consider all the relevant factors quickly and accurately.

Better time management. As mentioned above, less managerial time will be needed for the predictable things, and thus there is more time for dealing with unexpected events, threats and opportunities and for managing innovation and new and faster responses to new market opportunities or threats.

Speed is an important factor in today's economy. A good management system should allow managers to view data and assess key performance indicators (KPIs) whenever they need to do so, rather than having to wait for the next quarterly or monthly report. By that time, it may well be too late.

Greater flexibility. As noted above, flexibility is a key asset in the modern competitive environment. Companies have to be agile enough to respond to threats or opportunities when they appear. Management frameworks will free up expensive and scarce management time that is urgently needed to enable and support agile responses.

Potential weaknesses

We have argued that management frameworks are essential, but if the framework is badly designed or badly implemented, then things can certainly go wrong. One of the weaknesses of some earlier management frameworks, including some of the early strategic frameworks, is that they took a high level overview of strategy and organization, but failed to pay sufficient attention to detail. Others were good at reporting the details, but were lacking the overarching 'bigger picture' that would draw the organization together and allow cohesion to emerge from those details.

In Chapter 1, we drew an analogy between a management framework and the architecture of a house. It is easy to sit down and sketch a drawing of a beautiful house and then ask someone to build it and state that it should be high-comfort, well designed and low-cost. But questions will almost immediately arise. What do these objectives really mean? How can comfort be reconciled with low cost? Then practical problems begin to emerge. The plumber wants to know where the pipes for the plumbing are to go. The electrician wants to know where the plug points will be, where the cables will run, how many light fixtures there should be. The builder wants to know where the internal doors will be located. If these questions are not answered and these things are not done right, then the beautiful house will also be a dysfunctional house. That is why people involved in building projects use checklists and blueprints (frameworks/templates) to ensure things are not overlooked or missing or done in an inconsistent or incomplete way.

So it is with organizations. It is easy to say that we will have an organizational framework in the form of a hierarchical organization, or a matrix organization, or a virtual organization, but the task does not end there.

How are the various units/departments/people to be connected? How will the 'wiring' work to connect each in a clear, logical and easy-to-understand way, according to the principle of the 3Cs? Where will the lines of communication run? Who will report to whom, and how frequently, and in what format? What information will be collected and transmitted? What procedures will be followed? What controls are needed to ensure compliance and risk management? Too often, these things are left to evolve on their own. A management framework ensures that there are standard systems that cut right across the organization, ensuring consistent measurement, reporting, feedback and control. But this will not happen by itself. It needs to be designed into the plan through frameworks, hardwired into the total system.

That leads us to a second drawback, which is that badly designed and badly implemented management systems can be *too* rigid. Unlike a house, which can be converted to other uses only at significant expense and with difficulty, businesses have to be able to adapt quickly. A too-rigid management system hinders flexibility. This is one of the frequently observed problems with medium-term plans (MTPs). As has often been noted, by the time the MTP has been approved by the various committees who scrutinize it, it is already out of date. The world around us is affected by many, unknown forces leading to change, and each 'delta' causes multiple new deltas. There is no way of being certain about what will happen, no way of predicting everything. So adaptability and flexibility are key. Plans and the planning process should cater for that.

A third drawback is that the top-management focus of many, mostly non-aligned, frameworks means that business units and teams find them difficult to implement without direction from the top. Ideally, management frameworks should be implementable by anyone, although a degree of customization depending on the size and nature of the organization and the situation it is in will always be necessary.

A fourth drawback, and perhaps the most constraining factor, is that most managers are reluctant to give up their freedom to manage and communicate to their 'shop' in their own way. Contrary to managers and workers in manufacturing operations – or tradesmen building a house – managers in the 'white collar' part of the business often have problems adapting to and operating within more structured and integrated management processes.

If by now the reader has any doubts as to whether even simple management frameworks or templates have any purpose, or whether the benefits outweigh the negatives (like designing and using them), then let us make another analogy. When preparing to go travelling, which of these two methods is more efficient:

1. Packing your suitcase by just putting in the things you think you might need; or
2. Packing it by designing and using a *complete* and *consistent* checklist, in case for example you are going to a cold area and not to a warm destination?

If you follow the first method you might get angry that you have forgotten some small but important item like your razor or deodorant, or when walking out of a hotel into the cold that you forgot to bring a warm, thick scarf. But if you followed the second method, you would not only be more efficient but warmer, more comfortable and happier. In the end managers should at least try to be more efficient, not only for their own sake but also for the sake of the organization. Management frameworks can be a great tool for achieving this.

Building a management framework

This is beginning to look quite a tall order. How do we build a framework that is both holistic *and* pays attention to detail, is systematic *and* flexible, gives efficiency and control without stifling innovation and creativity? Since businesses and organizations are complex, then clearly management frameworks themselves will be fairly complex. We need to find a simple way of understanding them.

In order to design a 3Cs framework, we should have a clear understanding about what the elements and steps are that will lead from vision, mission, strategic priorities and the right organizational setting to total performance for all stakeholders. Building a management framework requires managers to *list* and *rank* all elements (drivers) that are involved in achieving performance goals. A holistic step-by-step approach is needed. Each step must be explicitly discussed before the framework is designed, if the framework itself is to be fit for purpose. It is these organizing steps that form the focus of the next chapter.

3
PLANNING FOR FRAMEWORKS

As we saw in Chapter 2, many different types of management frameworks and implementation approaches exist. The great majority of tools that are generally referred to as 'management frameworks' actually have very specific applications to just one type of managerial activity, for example the management of IT or human resources. These individual systems often do not connect well. Software-based systems, including enterprise resources management solutions like the ones from SAP or Oracle, provide a solid infrastructure but they do not substitute for management frameworks that are meant to dynamically interconnect the company's internal resources and capabilities with the external environment and assist managerial decision-making. We argue that any organization should have an over-arching management framework that encompasses the whole business, connects all the dots and ensures continuous and reliable communication and control from top to bottom, from centre to periphery.

It is also vitally important that management frameworks are seen as enabling mechanisms that add value to management by making managers better informed and more effective at what they do. This should result in a better run and more profitable business. However, if frameworks constrain managers and make them less effective, then the framework is actually subtracting value, making managers less efficient and potentially harming the company.

If a framework fails to be effective, then generally speaking one of two things has gone wrong. The first possibility is that the framework was badly designed and/or badly implemented and managers are not getting the information they need in order to make decisions and exercise control. It is important that frameworks are implemented carefully and thoroughly, just as it is important that an architect's plans are followed carefully when building a house. We will come on to this issue more fully later in the book.

The second possibility is that the framework, however well designed and implemented from a purely technical point of view, in fact does not support the organization's mission and purpose. One common problem is lack of integration between the different parts of the framework. As we noted too, within the broad management framework there are 'sub-frameworks' that relate to the activity of particular business units or business functions. When these sub-frameworks get out of alignment with the overall framework, problems very often result. The IT function might have developed ways of doing things that work very well from its own perspective, but simply are not aligned with the rest of the organization and its needs.

We can see this very clearly in the case of the National Health Service in the UK, which has as its primary purpose the delivery of effective health care to the British people. Over the course of the last two decades, the NHS has implemented a number of reporting and control frameworks with a view to cutting costs and making the organization more efficient. Many of these frameworks were based on ones already in use in the private sector, where they worked very well. But the health care service functions differently and has different resource requirements than other service sectors, and these frameworks did not take this into account. According to some reports, these frameworks have led to neither improvements in service and efficiency nor in lower costs. Indeed, in some cases the opposite has happened. In 2011, a major project designed to network hospitals and doctors' surgeries had to be abandoned after auditors concluded that the project would never work as designed, despite its immense cost.[1]

We come back again to the importance of 'connecting the dots'. For frameworks to really work effectively throughout an organization, management at every level across all units should be integrated to ensure connectedness and efficient and relevant information flow. The best way to do this is not to use a variety of bespoke frameworks and then somehow rope them together and hope they will work, as the National Health Service tried and failed to do. The best way is to use a single integrated framework designed to meet the needs of the organization. Such a framework should aim to capture all the major issues relating to the key domains of strategy, execution and organization. We call these issues 'drivers', because in everyday life managers need to deal with all of these issues, often simultaneously, and it is these issues that 'drive' the design and use of the framework, which in the end will allow the organization to reach its goals in an efficient way. For example, the need to build and maintain relationships with customers is a key management issue, something which occupies the attention not just of the marketing department but many different managers at various levels. Thus marketing is a 'driver', one of the drivers that needs to be taken into account when designing and using the framework.

Often too there are conflicts between the needs of different parts of the business, marketing and finance, IT and production. At a higher level there can be questions as to how a particular initiative fits into the overall strategy of the group. A single integrated management framework allows managers to understand these needs and move quickly to resolve conflicts.

A well-designed and implemented management framework which captures all the strategic, executional and organizational issues will make visible what has been invisible. Otherwise, there will be confusion within the organization about what should (or should not) be done and how to address the many conflicting or opposing (perceived or real) issues at hand.

Frameworks enable managers to gather information and get answers to questions. But unless we know the right questions to ask, then the answers we receive could be wrong, meaningless. Before implementing a framework, we need to go right back to the basics of the organization's strategy.

What does a management framework look like?

Let us now look at what a management framework would look like. Figure 3.1 shows the elements that need to go into a complete, overarching management framework.

The big picture of an overarching management framework

The first step is to establish the company's mission, vision and strategy and, more specifically, its strategic position, direction and priorities. After having defined these crucial elements of where the company wants to go, all actions necessary to achieve those goals can be grouped as part of six drivers. They are called 'drivers' because they drive the entire company

FIGURE 3.1 Comprehensive, complete, consistent

from mission, vision and strategy to ultimate performance. The emphasis here is on *overall* excellence or *total excellence* (like total football). It is not good enough to simply be good at one specific thing. Too often, a company's strategy is based on just one driver. For example, a company might aim for 'operational excellence'. But why just that? Why not marketing excellence or financial excellence or any other activity?

These six drivers are fundamentally aligned and the execution level elements of each of the six drivers of excellence have to be specified by the people involved and responsible for the respective functions. For example, the organizational drivers will be determined according to the overall goals of top management. It will then be fine-tuned and completed by the HR team. The HR managers at head office, business units and regions/countries will all have input. The same is true for all the other drivers as well. The entire planning, budgeting and feedback system (including what auditors and controllers report back) needs to be part of the overarching framework, as does the sharing of knowledge and internal and external communication.

Finally, an overarching integrity management approach has to be part of the execution. What we mean by integrity management is the 'how to' question. While the six drivers directly drive performance along the 'what to do' question, integrity management assures that the right things are done the right way.

We will discuss how all these framework elements connect specifically, in subsequent chapters. This chapter concentrates on the vital first steps including, mission, vision and strategic direction. We will also discuss the purpose and scope of the framework, who should have responsibility for the framework, who should drive the process through, how it should be implemented and how it will work in an integrated fashion, and how it should be adapted over time. By the end of this chapter, readers should have a better understanding of how frameworks function and what the critical priorities are. We will then go on to discuss those priorities in more detail in succeeding chapters.

Mission and vision

Every good company, large or small, has a clearly articulated and well understood mission and vision. One of the tasks of leadership is to make certain the mission and vision are clearly articulated and understood by everyone in the organization.[2] They should be simple and to the point, and should not be a kind of short strategic plan as is the case in some companies.

An organization's *mission* represents its purpose, its reason for being.[3] What was it established to do? What does it see as being its primary function? The National Health Service in Britain believes its mission is to be a provider of high-quality health care to people who need it. Apple's mission is to provide high-quality electronics goods that will enrich people's lives. Google's mission is to provide a service that helps people gain access to information around the world. The mission of India's Tata group is to create prosperity and help strengthen the communities in which it operates. The mission of ING Asia Pacific is to be customers' preferred choice in its chosen markets.

Vision refers to the future of the organizations and its stretch goal. Ideally it should communicate the areas where the company believes it has good prospects for a successful future. An organization might have a vision of becoming the leader in its own business sector, or of pioneering new markets in Asia or Latin America, or of becoming a leader in the development of a particular new technology. Microsoft's vision is to remain the leader in the global software industry by constantly innovating new products and staying ahead of the competition. Tesco's vision is to expand its reach and become a truly global retailer. Rolls-Royce's motors vision is to build the world's most prestigious cars, and so on. While the vision describes a stretch goal it does not set specific quantitative targets. It forms the basis for these quantifiable goals.

Taken together, the mission and vision of an orgainzation help to point the company in the direction it needs to be going. In theory, all the company's efforts should be focused on fulfilling the mission and vision.[4] One of the key objectives of management frameworks is to enable management to carry out the mission and fulfil the vision more effectively, in a structured and logical way, rather than using ad hoc, 'seat of the pants' methods. A framework should help to focus energies and thinking on the mission and vision.

Again, it is important that the organization should share a single mission and vision. There is debate over how strong and focused the mission and vision should be, and in their recent study *Great by Choice*, Jim Collins and Morten Hansen discovered that companies that are successful over the long run often have rather general and often seemingly unfocused mission statements and grand, all encompassing vision statements. In other words, while those companies define their general purpose, they seem to deliberately keep these able to evolve.[5] But whether the mission is phrased in a highly focused way, for example 'we aim to be the world's leading maker of precision instruments', or unfocused, for example 'we aim to create satisfied customers', the main point to remember is that everyone throughout the organization should share a belief and common understanding of the mission and vision. This will set the basis for everyone pulling in the same direction. If executives and employees do not pull together, then there is also very little chance of implementing a management framework effectively. If there are too many different beliefs, too many different factions trying to manage the organization their own way, this will pull the framework apart. Remember, frameworks are not a substitute for management actions. They are a tool to help make managers more effective but, like all tools, they can be compromised.

BOX 3.1 BEST FIT?

Recently a CEO/owner of a succesful company was asked by a journalist about which factors contributed to the success of the company. The CEO answered: 'From the beginning, I have had a vision to be number one through innnovation, creativity, and efficiency. I have five strategies for achieving growth: protect the environment, conserve energy, produce high-quality product, invest in the best technology, and find the best human resources.' Looking at the surface, you would say that this sounds a good vision and good strategy. But wouldn't the vision statement fit better in a 'mission' statement, while the strategy would fit better under 'strategic priorities'?

Strategic position and direction

Having determined the company's mission and vision, management then has to discuss and decide on the strategy that will be followed in order to deliver on the objectives of the mission and vision statements. While these statements might be quite high level and abstract, defining the strategy allows managers to be more clear regarding execution choices and specific decisions. Anecdotally, everybody has heard the statement that if you ask ten managers 'What is the company's strategy?', you will get ten different answers. Worse, if you ask the same manager the question again, you are likely to get a different answer. People are not good at remembering what has been agreed or what they said or were told before. Typically they are able to share some simple statements such as 'focus on the customer' or 'be number one' or ' improve cost/income ratio'. But in real life, building successful competitive businesses is much more complex and challenging than these simple phrases suggest.

There are many different definitions of business strategy, ranging from the rational and formal approach known as the 'planning school', popularized by Kenneth Andrews and others, to the 'emergent school' developed by Henry Mintzberg, the 'learning school', the 'resource-based school', the 'positioning school' and so on.[6] Space precludes a full discussion of these schools here. In any case, the basic principles set out here are relevant to all forms of strategic thinking from planned to emergent, with the caveat that some adaptation of these principles may be required depending on which school of strategic thinking is being followed.

Yet this very large body of literature on business strategy, and the plethora of ideas about what strategy is, have not really helped lead to greater understanding at the managerial level. As Profesor Richard Rumult of UCLA explains, 'Most of the world isn't intending to get strategy wrong: they aren't getting it at all.' Most strategies are a 'superficial restatement of the obvious combined with a generous sprinkling of buzzwords'.[7] Research by scholars at the Thunderbird School of Global Management mentioned earlier showed that even top companies have problems in communicating clearly and consistently what their strategy is. At ING Asia Pacific similar things took place. When the CEOs of the twenty business units were asked what their strategy was, it soon became evident that most people did not have any idea of how to best articulate the notion of strategy.

Figure 3.2 captures the key ingredients of any strategy along five major dimensions, including business lines, geographic reach, products, distribution channels and customer groups. We call this the spider chart, which has been developed based on a concept initially introduced by the consultants of Bain & Co. The template allows managers to better understand and communicate where the core of their business is today. This describes the present strategic *position*, the starting point of the framework development process. Most companies, apart from start-ups, will have a position which can be further defined using the model shown in Figure 3.2. This five-dimension model allows managers to identify potential misalignments between these elements. For example, is our distribution system developed to reach the maximum number of our target customers' groups? Once this is known, data useful to determining future strategic direction can be plotted onto the chart shown in Figure 3.3. This chart brings in some action-specificity and understanding of potential resources gaps.

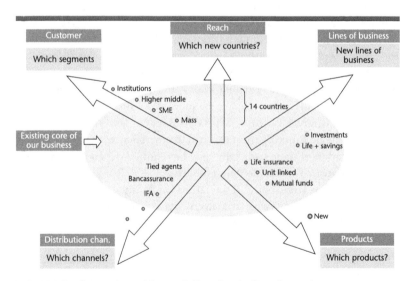

FIGURE 3.2   Strategic position and direction in five dimensions

Source: ING Asia Pacific, Bain & Co.

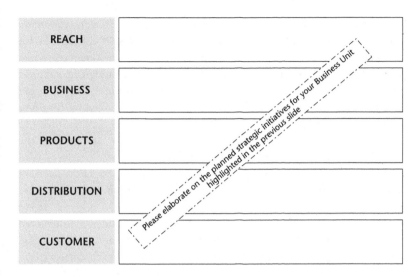

FIGURE 3.3 Further explanation of strategic direction

The key point is that no matter which approach is being used, an understanding of the mission and vision of the company is an essential prerequisite to defining the company's strategic direction. All discussions about strategy require consideration of the five key elements of strategic direction. Further, all five elements are interdependent to a large extent and cannot be determined in isolation.

Reach refers to the company's presence in particular markets. In what geographical markets does it currently operate? From this point managers can begin to understand whether there is a need to expand into specific markets, or to withdraw from or consolidate others. The need to expand – or contract – can be driven by opportunities: for example, expanding into Asian markets could be very profitable. Or it might be driven by threats: for example, if we do not expand into Asian markets now, then our competitors will do so and it will be harder for us to get a foothold there in coming years. Or perhaps our home market is shrinking and thus if we want to secure future performance, we have to move into growth markets overseas.

Business refers to the lines of business the company is in, or should be in. For example, a financial institution might be in the businesses of savings, loans, insurance, pension plans or asset and wealth management. Marks &

Spencer is engaged in food and clothing retailing and even in real estate. Some companies might focus tightly on one business (McDonald's with restaurants), or be widely dispersed over many different segments like General Electric or Samsung from Korea. When considering strategic direction, one should think about whether the company is in the right business areas to support its mission and vision (we will come to this point again in Chapter 4).

Products follows naturally on from the line of business, and refers to the range of products (for the purposes of this discussion, 'products' also includes services) the company offers. Do these products meet the needs of customers? Can we competitively and profitably produce and sell these products?

Distribution refers to the channels through which products are delivered to customers. Does the company sell direct to its customers, or does it use agents or other middlemen? The choice of distribution channel will be different for each company depending on the type of business – McDonald's' main channel of distribution is through its restaurants (owned or franchised), Amazon.com uses a combination of the Internet to allow customers to make purchases and then physical distribution through couriers and the postal system. Within large businesses there will be differences again across different business units. Again, implicit in both these elements is the need to examine the status quo and determine whether the product offering and the distribution system are designed to meet customer needs and to help the company to carry out its mission and fulfil its vision.

Last but far from least, there are *customers*. The company needs to consider its existing customer segments, and ask if there are other segments that need to be reached. Should we have more customers, or fewer? Should we be looking at other groups such as youth, women, minorities, and trying to attract them? Most importantly do we have the right customers to help us fulfil our mission and vision? One American accounting firm suddenly realized that a customer segment which it had served for years, when the time devoted to dealing with this segment was compared to the income generated, was not actually profitable.[8] The company moved away from serving this segment and concentrated on others it could serve more effectively and with a greater revenue potential.

So far, so good. To those familiar with the literature on strategy, none of this will seem very unusual. These are the basic strategic considerations that every business has to take into account, all the time. But there is a further important consideration that has to be taken into account. All of these five issues – reach, lines of business, products, distribution and customers – have to be aligned with each other. As noted above, there are a number of inter-dependencies between these five dimensions of strategy. It is no use deciding that a company will serve a particular customer segment if it lacks the products to appeal to them or the proper channels to reach and support customers efficiently. There is thus a constant strategic tension between what customers want, what the business needs to do in order to reach them, and what it actually can do. No business can do what every potential customer wants all the time. There comes a point when managers need to look at what we call 'satisficing': doing the best they can with the resources available to meet the needs of the most important customers.

Strategic priorities

Analysing the issues discussed above and agreeing on the strategic position and directions should provide a roadmap showing where we are now and where we are going. This analysis should aim to create a specific list of concrete strategic issues (for example, we will open offices in three new countries and five new cities in the next year), or 'drivers'. Figure 3.4 categorizes these drivers into six key groups.

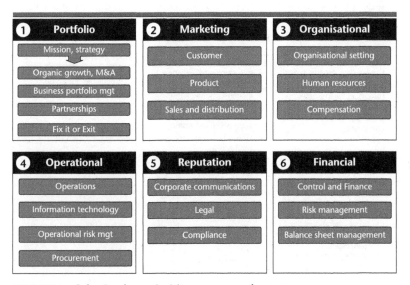

FIGURE 3.4   Selecting key priorities to execute the strategy

Figure 3.4 shows a finer level of granularity within each of the six main drivers. While they are still quite generic and intuitive they function as a 'how to' menu for managers, that can be further specified. To demonstrate what this could mean in practice, we provide an example in Figure 3.5.

What becomes clear at once from Figures 3.1 and 3.5 is that we want to achieve *overall* performance excellence. The idea that overall excellence can be achieved by focusing on just three or four priorities, as so many managers often do, is simply wrong. Other priorities, if not taken into account during the planning stage, might seriousely threaten the implementation phase. For example, what is the point of not making finance a priority if the orgainzation runs out of funds to support particular projects? If IT systems are not a priority, then what happens when those systems break down, as experienced by BlackBerry maker Research in Motion?

The general strategic roadmap gives us the helicopter perspective. But just as an architectural design does not show all the relevant details that the craftsmen who build a house really need, our roadmap does not show all of the details we need for successful strategy implementation. However, we should not have to look very far to find those details; they almost certainly already exist within the organization. The problem usually is that these details are not obvious. Often they are overshadowed by a short-term

Portfolio	Marketing	Organizational
1. Double digit organic growth	4. Introduce profitable new product offerings	8. Expand organisational capabilities, including management development
2. Active portfolio management (M&A), including better allocation of capital	5. Increase profitable multi-channel sales	9. Improve performance culture
3. More and stronger partnerships	6. Develop strategy for youngsters and women	
	7. Strengthen customer satisfaction	

Operational	Reputation	Financial
10. Increase efficiency and distributor/customer satisfaction	13. Increase brand recognition	17. Raise $ capital + debt
11. Improve operational risk management	14. Strengthen compliance	18. Expand value-based management
12. Obtain/maintain satisfactory audit rating	15. Communicate clearly to internal/external stakeholders	19. Strengthen risk mgt
	16. Ensure integrity, ethical behaviour in all areas	20. Improve MIS & control

FIGURE 3.5 Strategic priorities

tactical managerial mindset. But even if these details exist explicitly in manuals, reports and strategic planning documents, and are remembered, they might not be aligned with the overall plan because the individuals who wrote them were working in isolation, in silos disconnected from the rest of the organization. When a composer writes music, they specify exactly when the various musicians have to play which notes on which instruments. Unfortunately, most strategic plans are not so well coordinated.

In order to capture still more detail, we can cascade the levels of detail down further. Figure 3.6 shows as an example the sub-template of the marketing driver, with 'customer segment' as the sub-driver.

Here is how the template works. On the top right hand corner we see a little conceptual diagram that shows which driver we are discussing (highlighted) as part of the overall six main driver roadmap.

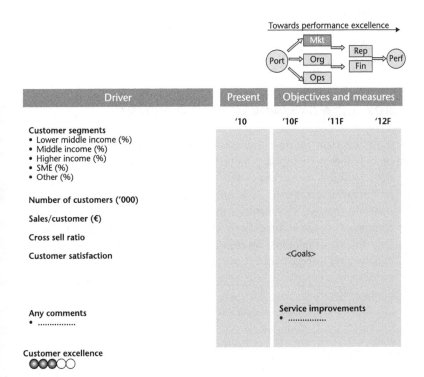

FIGURE 3.6 Customer segments

At the bottom left side there are five small circles which can be coloured to reflect assessment of the amount/quality of progress that has been made in terms of achieving specific goals. The scoring tool helps us to make sub-driver performance comparable to other sub-drivers. These scores (which are set at each sub-'page') will be the input for:

1. Measuring where we stand and the quality of the specific item/depart-ment. Then, when all of these are added together, this tells us the status of the whole organization. This is very important input for the various internal and external control and audit functions, or even supervisors when they are required to verify and give an opinion about the quality of the company.
2. Determining which objectives and KPIs apply to managers responsible for a certain area or function. In the past this process was sometimes referred to as management by objectives. Moreover, this will allow the organization to link these objectives and to set targets for pay-for-performance metrics and bonuses. With the management framework in place, this trivial and sensitive issue becomes much more objective and transparent.

BOX 3.2 A DYNAMIC LIVING DOCUMENT

It will be clear by now that within the framework implementation process things should and indeed must be well aligned. All of the dots must be connected if the organization is to achieve overall performance excellence. It is critical to understand that this is a dynamic process. Old items – things which have been done and completed – need to be deleted, and new ones have to be added as they emerge as relevant. We regard an ideal management framework as a dynamic living document *and process*. Only this perspective allows us to address internal or external issues in real time and to allow us to operate effectively.

The drivers

The six sets of drivers identified in Figure 3.5 help us to zero in on what has to be done. They help us to understand the strategy formulation and implementation needs of the organization and its stakeholders and the key tasks that need to be performed in order to achieve its mission. They define the direction that strategic thinking needs to follow. They also map out which elements need to be included in an organization's specific framework. To continue with our metaphor, these drivers are the 'dots' that when connected will lead to performance excellence. Strategy conceptually connects them; the management framework then makes those connections tangible for strategy implementation.

Let us now consider each set of drivers one-by-one.

The *portfolio* drivers reflect directly back to organizational mission and vision by focusing on how the company will grow (or indeed, in times of a downturn, how it will contract). For example, if we want to grow will this be through organic growth, acquisitions or strategic partnerships? Will it grow by adding new markets (i.e. entering new countries or developing new business lines)? McDonald's has just a single business line, fast food restaurants. Yet management could decide to add another line of business by separating all the real estate it owns into a new business line, property management. It could then appoint management to drive this business unit forward with the fast-food business unit as its main in-house customer, with a service-level agreement at a cost price-plus basis. This was in fact done by European budget clothing retailer C&A some years ago when it created an in-group unit for managing its extensive property portfolio.

The *marketing* driver focuses on customers, sales and distribution. What will we sell, to whom, and how? How do we manage and align the interdependencies between product, customer and distribution?

The *operational* driver tells us how the strategic and related tasks will be carried out from an operational dimension. Where will operations be located and how structured? How will the supply chain be managed? What if anything will be outsourced? What technology, including IT, will be required to support operations? What operational risk factors need to be managed?

The *organizational* driver tells us who will carry out all of the primary and support activities. How will the organization be structured? Will we have a hierarchical organization, or a matrix? What are the human resources requirements? What compensation will they need? What are their training and management development requirements? Who will report to whom and how often? How will people be managed and incentivized? In strategy textbooks the operational and organizational functions are often referred to as structure. However, very few books go into detail when it comes to explaining structure, and even fewer describe how organizational structure is actually connected with the other dots. The result is that strategy and structure are often disconnected.

The *reputational* driver focuses on how the company will maintain its reputation and its brand. It sets out the role to be played by corporate communications, both internal and external, and also reminds everyone of the legal issues and how compliance will be enforced. It considers issues such as ethics, environmental impact, and reputation for honesty and moral behaviour. Reputational failures can seriously damage a company's chances of successfully executing its strategy.

Finally, the *financial* driver focuses on finance functions including financial reporting and control, treasury, cash flow, balance sheet and risk management. Issues include the timely and adequate provision of management information, and auditing and regulatory reporting.

The framework model (Figure 3.1) also includes another overarching performance excellence dimension, which we call integrity management. In recent years integrity and compliance management has developed beyond being a reactive and rather static mitigation activity for correcting or minimizing negative effects from managerial misconduct, to an active tool that is being used to assure long term organizational sustainability.[9] Today, leading corporations use integrity and compliance management approaches that proactively influence organizational core processes and employee behaviours. The questions that need to be asked include not only 'What has been achieved?' but also 'How has it been achieved?' Performance excellence is important, but if unreasonable amounts of resources have been used to reach the prescribed performance goals or if any stakeholder, including employees, partners or external members of society at large, have been negatively affected, then performance excellence will not be sustainable. Many leading firms recognize this and develop smart integrity management systems into their processes.

The role of the management framework

Our six drivers are nothing new. In essence every company, no matter where it is located or how big or small it is, has to deal with these six drivers, every day, all of the time. The task of management is to respond to these drivers and create and execute strategies that take these drivers into account and help the company to carry out its mission.

BOX 3.3 PERILS OF OVER-FOCUS ON ONE DRIVER

'Documents unlock bank's strategy failures' was the headline of an article in the *Financial Times* on 22 April 2008, shortly after the financial crisis began to gather momentum. The article concerned UBS, which had to raise new capital to fund an $18.7 billion write-down on a number of assets which the bank had 'unexpectedly' on its books. In a meeting with investors it was explained that 'the investment bank was focused on the maximization of revenue'. The *Financial Times* article drew particular attention to the fact that UBS management did not raise concerns as to whether systems and staff could cope with the rate of growth of the business. The report also mentioned that 'the compensation structure generally made little recognition of risk issues or adjustment for risk/other qualitative indicators'.

This is a sad but useful example of a company focusing too much on one 'driver' (revenues) but not able to manage *all* the other key strategic drivers, such as risk management, reporting and control and well-balanced incentive schemes.

As we described in Chapter 1, it is very difficult for the leaders of a large corporation to know what is going on in every corner of their business. Leaders needs tools to help them monitor, measure and understand. That is where the management framework comes in. It supports the strategy and structure during the strategy implementation process. Through the framework, everyone can understand intended outcomes of the strategy, at the corporate, business unit and individual level. More importantly still, the framework helps managers at all levels to have insight and access into each others' tasks and goals. Knowing what is going on in the organization around them will help managers to integrate their work with that of colleagues and therefore function more effectively. Consequently, some of the functions of the framework are to break down silos and make visible the process to connect all relevant drivers in getting to sustainable performance.

We have been talking so far about large companies, but small companies need frameworks too. Small companies may not be as organizationally complex as large ones, or have the geographical reach; however, they also often do not have the same managerial resources as large companies. Environ (not its real name), a small manufacturing company in the southeast of

England, has just over 100 employees and a turnover of £7.2 million. Some of its staff is located at its headquarters, but others – supply chain staff, sales managers and the like – operate in the field. Headquarters consists of a managing director and two other full-time directors and two full-time administrative staff plus some part-timers. The factory is also located in the same location. The managing director freely admits that he finds it difficult to follow events in the company on a day-to-day basis. Things happen so quickly that he finds he is spending most of his time reacting, with very little time to plan and be proactive. A management framework that captures and specifies all the things the organization needs to do and all the things on which he himself needs to concentrate would help to simplify his business and make the management task less complex. The managing director would become a more effective manager as a result, and his company would become more efficient in its use of resources and information.

Establishing the scope of the framework

It should now be clear why we argue that every venture needs one – and only one – *overarching management framework* which covers the entire organization. It is important that this framework includes every part of the organization and every function. The functional frameworks that we introduced in Chapter 2 accomplish this only to a limited extent. They can be very useful for managing particular tasks, but they cover only parts of the organization or they do not reach deep enough in order to connect all the different organizational elements effectively. As a result, they do not help us towards our first priority, which is the management of complexity.

It becomes evident that those functional frameworks need to connect with the overarching management framework. For example, financial reporting and control frameworks used by the finance department must be fully compatible with the overarching management framework. Most companies apply frameworks for financial reporting, mostly in the form of preset financial spreadsheets. Yet finance is basically the only department that applies such standardized frameworks. What if other units and departments were to follow this good example, even when done in a more qualitative format? The company would then get closer to developing a full list of things to be done. The Balanced Scorecard, as introduced in Chapter 2, is one tool to capture these qualitative data, albeit without a structured integration logic.[10] Once all information has been collected from all departments and business units, it then becomes possible to align and enable them to work together more effectively.

This is the first step to breaking down the walls between silos. Free flow of information leads to transparency for everybody and about everything. But again, to repeat the earlier point, this cannot be achieved if everyone is using different frameworks, because incompatibilities between frameworks mean that managers end up unable to communicate with each other. Especially in large and complex companies with many different business units and many layers of organization, it is crucial that managers have a single common management framework to enable communication.

Who has responsibility for the framework?

It is vitally important that all layers of management are involved in developing the framework and implementing the agreed upon objectives along comparable measures in an integrated and simple manner. Figure 3.7, which shows the Total Performance Excellence (TPE) framework developed at ING Asia Pacific, illustrates how a well-designed framework can provide everyone with a 'bird's eye view' of what is in place in all parts of the organization and how their activities fit into the greater scheme of things.

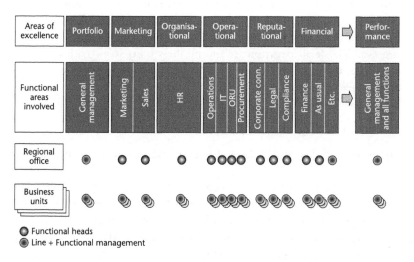

FIGURE 3.7 Managing the TPE framework

An integrated framework allows managers to be instantly updated on progress on each of the six drivers and where the company stands in terms of meeting its targets. Executives can then focus on all of the issues relevant to driving performance and not just single issues such as sales, cost management, or operational excellence.

Leaders are responsible for choosing and adapting the framework, but others are responsible for implementation and making it work. Once the need for a framework is clearly understood, it is the responsibility of leadership to take the initiative and start the process of implementing and introducing the framework. The first task is usually to explain clearly why and how a framework will address the flaws and shortcomings in the ways the company is now being managed. The leader should engage fully and be backed up by the relevant managers and specialists who can help coach other managers and explain further the benefits. All of this will help to achieve organizational 'buy-in'. People will be more likely to put their shoulders to the wheel and help implement the framework if they understand clearly the benefits of doing so.

At the same time, however, the framework will only work if everyone in the organization plays their part in making it work. This means, for example, that when designing and 'populating' the templates with data (activities, objectives, key performance indicators) people must take ownership and feel responsible for their domain of activity. For example, if corporate marketing sees an opportunity to push up sales by 3 per cent across all European countries, it should engage fully with the business units in these countries but it should engage also with the financial, operational and organizational departments in order to assure that the needed resources are available. If all departments and business units work with the same templates, the process of alignment of resources and needs becomes much less complex and more coherent.

How will the framework be implemented?

In his book *Making Strategy Work*, Lawrence Hrebiniak comments that

> execution is critical to success. Execution represents a disciplined process or a logical set of connected activities that enables an organization to take a strategy and make it work. Without a careful, planned approach to execution, strategic goals cannot be attained. Developing such a logical approach, however, represents a formidable challenge to management.[11]

Implementing an overarching management framework, as with any aspect of strategy, requires first that leadership thinks carefully about what the framework is intended to do and how it will support business activities, and second, that the implementation of the framework is carefully planned. Action plans must be drawn up for each business unit or staff unit, at all levels from the boardroom to the shop floor. These must be communicated and all staff involved briefed carefully as to their own role and what is expected of them. A general instruction to 'just get on with it' will not be enough. Vagueness and imprecision have no place here.

How will the framework be adapted over time?

Periodically managers will be asked to update and adapt their views and the facts of what is going on and what should be going on. A set of templates needs to be designed to facilitate a 3Cs (comprehensive, complete, consistent) sharing of the relevant information and process models. In order to refresh each manager's memory, the original objectives should first be rehearsed. Each business and functional manager can then add the 'progress' he or she has made and any issues that should be shared and discussed. (Figure 3.8

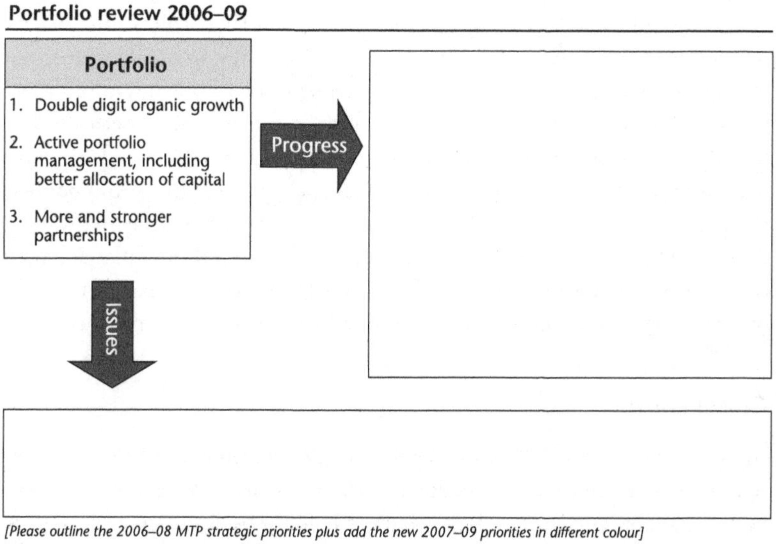

Portfolio review 2006–09

[Please outline the 2006–08 MTP strategic priorities plus add the new 2007–09 priorities in different colour]

FIGURE 3.8 Portfolio review

gives an example of this process relating to the portfolio driver.) Based on this input, managers can then discuss and decide efficiently what needs to be adapted. The advantage is that everybody is immediately on the same page and understands the elements that are interconnected across functional or geographical domains. The framework provides the unifying language for managers to coordinate their tasks and more.

It is important that the 3Cs principle be followed over time. For example, a business unit executive has stated that it is her goal to become a local market leader. Under the portfolio section of the framework, she should be required to explain how that growth will be achieved specifically. Does she plan to make acquisitions? If so, she should provide details and financially measurable objectives. Does she plan to establish new partnerships or add to existing ones? Does she have to fix or close non-performing departments or will she just grow organically? What specific actions does she plan to take and where (in the call centre, front office, products, channels, etc.), and along what timelines? What will this growth require in terms of HR, operational support, IT, financial investment, and so on?

Using a management framework which follows the 3Cs principle allows an organization to become adaptive, flexible and efficient/effective all at the same time. As we discussed in Chapter 1, more and more managers have to move in and out of the ambiguous zones that make their jobs more and more complex and unpredictable. Too often their robust but strictly defined plans are already 'outdated' even before they have been approved by top management. Too often also, managers insist on believing in these plans and sticking to them regardless of their effectiveness, because they naively believe that it is possible to predict the future. This leads them to deny tomorrow's realities in terms of risks and opportunities. And because their plans do not follow the 3Cs principle, they often lack many vital details which are necessary for success. Overarching management frameworks of the kind we are discussing here allow managers to adapt dynamically and flexibly to the realities that tomorrow will bring.

Conclusion

In this chapter, we saw how management frameworks are in effect strategic roadmaps with the tools embedded in the templates. *A management framework is not a goal in itself.* It is a means of helping to make choices, setting direction and priorities based on an organization's capabilities and resources to enable it to achieve its strategic goals.

.

We saw too why an overarching management framework has to reflect every important strategic issue, not just some. A company's operational efficiency, marketing effectiveness, financial viability, reputation and image, and so on, are all intimately interconnected. An overarching management framework recognizes this interconnection and reflects it. It allows managers to understand what is going on everywhere in the organization and make connections. This will lead to the breaking down of silos, which will lead to effectively managing the organization as a seamless whole.

In the following chapters we will look at each set of drivers in detail and explain how they interconnect with other drivers.

4

THE PORTFOLIO DRIVER

One of the most important aspects of strategy formulation and implementation involves determining how growth (or in some cases, downsizing) will be achieved. Questions that need to be asked under the heading of the portfolio driver concern issues such as expansion through organic growth, partnerships, mergers and acquisition (M&A) or expanding into new product/service lines and new geographical markets. In some cases these decisions might involve reducing activities in particular areas, by closing or selling some business units and withdrawing from some areas. Having answered these questions, the next step is to add detail to each point, as we discuss below.

BOX 4.1 PORTFOLIO DRIVERS

Organic growth v. M&A
Business portfolio management
Partnerships
Fix it or exit/outsource

In this chapter we will examine the first of the six sets of drivers in more detail. As well as unpicking the different aspects of this driver and showing how and why they are relevant and need to be included in the framework, we will also discuss the critical issues of interdependence; that is, how each set of drivers relates to the others. This should provide insights into ways of breaking down silos and establishing a framework that builds strong lateral as well as vertical communications.

Portfolio drivers comprise a set of strategic priorities that relate to growth (assuming the company wants to grow, as most companies do). If we look back at Chapter 3, we see that growth can be achieved by expanding on all five dimensions, for example by adding countries or cities (reach) or adding new business lines. Consider for example how Samsung has moved from a business line in television sets into new ones such as mobile phones. Samsung has also expanded internationally, entering the North American and European markets and then other markets around the world. Other companies can and do expand in much the same way by launching new products or adding new distribution channels and customer segments, as we discussed in Chapter 3. So the first key question is: How will managers grow the company? Or, if certain business units are not performing well or when things are going badly wrong in the business environment, as happened in 2008–9 for example, how will they downsize in order to protect the core of the company and keep it going?

How does a company grow? Conventional wisdom says there are only two ways, through organic growth or through M&A. In some cases, particularly in certain geographical regions, other methods such as partnerships and joint ventures may be called for. In fact, many companies use a combination of portfolio strategies, depending on the markets they are in, the nature of competition and regulation, and their own size and resources. It follows that a management framework will have to be capable of supporting a wide range of growth options, and often several options at the same time.

Getting from here to there

In the course of planning the strategic growth of the company, a great deal of value can be created – or destroyed – depending on how well and how proactively the portfolio drivers are managed. In reality, few companies capture and describe well their strategic intent in ways that make clear how these portfolio drivers impact on the business. In Chapter 3, we saw how strategy is clearly framed in the context of the corporate mission and goals. Companies are sometimes very good at outlining their plans in terms of marketing (see Chapter 5) and operations (see Chapter 7), but unless those plans have been properly contextualized within the wider strategic goals, then we miss important initiatives (drivers) or once again encounter the danger of silos going their own separate ways and the business as a whole drifting away from its strategic ends. On top of this, management needs to ensure that all the drivers are part of the bigger overarching framework.

It is critical to start from the beginning, and rehearse once again just exactly what the vision and mission are, and remember what happens when these are out of alignment with the strategy. Consider the case of Danish toymaker Lego Group, which has one of the most well-known brands in the world. From its foundation, Lego's mission was to make educational toys which children – and some adults – all around the world could use. Growth was organic, and came mostly from adding new product lines and expanding into new markets. But in 2000, Lego's leadership had a rush of blood to the head. They began expanding by adding new lines of business (and therefore new business units), getting into new sectors such as film and video. Lego had departed from its mission and its founding vision. The result was sudden and heavy losses, the first in the company's history. To restore order, the company divested itself of many of these non-core new ventures and began to concentrate once more on making and marketing educational toys. Within a few years, it had returned to profit once more.

We have seen many other examples of such companies in the past – Royal Ahold, the Dutch supermarket chain which expanded rapidly in all directions (including major expansions in the USA and Brazil) until it imploded; Nortel, the Canadian telecoms company which embarked on an acquisitions spree so highly leveraged that it created a bubble within the company; and so on – where growth was seemingly at random, growth for growth's sake. There was no transparency as to how growth was to be achieved. There was no coherent growth strategy, no evidence of a logical choice of organic growth or growth through M&A. Often in such cases too there is no strategy for divestment. Companies need to grow, of course, but they must do so in ways that are in line with their vision and mission, and even more importantly, in line with their existing and future capabilities. Successful growth, in the words of consultants at Bain & Co., requires companies to 'leverage the core'.[1]

Logically, if a company already has competitive skills in one area, it will be much easier to leverage these capabilities by moving into related areas. For example, Nike's expertise in making soccer kit will enable the company to move more easily into making, for example, basketball kit than to move into the film business. Nike has been very successful at leveraging its production and marketing skills around the world. It grew by expanding along the five dimensions shown in the 'spider chart': customers, reach, lines of business, channels and products. In contrast, when the successful car manufacturer Mercedes Benz decided to move into aircraft production, the company quickly found that this move took it too far from its core capabilities.

Another option can be to *partner* with other companies that possess the desired skills and competencies. For example, when ING wanted to get access to large numbers of bank clients in Asian countries in order to sell insurance and investment products, it entered into many partnerships with local banks. Small stakes were taken in some of these banks in order to build distribution partnerships in China (with the Bank of Beijing), Korea (Kookmin Bank) and India (Vysya Bank). Yet partnerships too can be risky, and should only be entered into if they genuinely suit the needs of the business and are very well managed and maintained.

To sum up, no matter what means they use, managers who understand and actively manage the portfolio driver can create shareholder value. Interestingly, and perhaps somewhat worryingly, many of the management frameworks we discussed in Chapter 2 do not assist managers to manage their portfolios in this way. And yet this is a vital element in strategic execution, and good portfolio management is essential in driving a strategy through to completion.

The portfolio dimension

Management at the various layers and business units has to 'check' a couple of boxes relating to this driver when specifying their strategic direction, as follows:

1.   Organic growth (or downsizing)?
2.   Acquisition, mergers or disinvestments?
3.   Adding/exiting lines of businesses/countries?
4.   Expanding or adding new partnerships?
5.   Weak performing business units to be fixed or closed?

Obviously the answers to each of above points can vary per business unit. But finding those answers must start with the overall direction and guidance of the business. Does this business want to grow, and if so in which direction and how? Clarity and transparency on these issues is crucial. Otherwise, each business unit and department which looks at these questions is likely to come up with different answers, and then instead of pulling together the business is likely to fall apart. The first task is to make sure that all the relevant questions are listed. The second is to make sure that each is well answered, in a way that the data are sorted out and categorized in a logical way.

BOX 4.2 CONNECTING THE DOTS . . .

How portfolio drivers impact on other drivers

Marketing drivers: Portfolio drivers make it clear how, where and when the company will grow and expand (or if necessary, contract). This helps to give the marketing department its frame of reference. For example, if it is decided that the company will grow organically, marketing knows that the key task is to increase sales of existing and new products, channels and/or customer groups. If there is to be a programme of mergers, then marketing will have to take a range of existing products and services and integrate them with existing offerings.

Organizational drivers: The form the organization takes depends to an extent on the strategic direction the business intends to follow (see Chapter 6). The organization must be fit for its intended purpose. Organic growth will require organic expansion of the organization with perhaps the creation of new business units; mergers or acquisitions require that new entities have to be integrated into the existing organizational structure; partnerships require effective mechanisms for managing and communicating with partners, and so on.

Operational drivers: Partnerships, M&A and organic growth each have their own challenges in terms of operations management. For example, in the case of an acquisition, will the back offices or call centres of each company be integrated or left as they are? Knowing how the company intends to proceed in general strategic terms helps operations managers to define their own tasks.

Reputational drivers: If there is an acquisition or new partnership, or if the compnany decides to exit a particular country, then the internal and external communications functions need to be aligned with this process. Stakeholder groups will inevitably ask questions, and these must be answered. Legal aspects must also be dealt with early on. For example, will an M&A require the formation of a new holding company?

Financial drivers: How will growth, whether organically or through M&A, be financed? What will this mean for the company's credit rating, solvency and liquidity position? How will MIS be integrated? These and other aspects are important 'dots' for the finance department to consider and connect to.

As soon as all business units within the company have shared the relevant data from the portfolio drivers, it is then relatively simple for management to start comparing the data in order to get a full picture. It is then possible to see how the company is intending to grow, where organic growth will occur, where there will be acquisitions and partnerships, what rates of growth are expected and what the estimated costs will be. Alternatively, if capital constraints mean that the company can only grow organically, or even must contract, the data from the portfolio templates of each business unit will show which business units are adhering to policy and which are not. This gives managers a 'helicopter view' which shows them where the entire company is heading.

This process also gives managers information (or at least an indication) about the total sum of capital needed for acquisitions, partnerships or internal investment (capital which will be supplied when they come to consider the *financial* driver). Similarly, managers can see how much capital will be freed up by selling or closing down certain business units. Finally, as well as providing information for top management, portfolio drivers help to describe to both internal and external stakeholders what the portfolio is, and how it will be expanded and developed in line with overall strategy.

Options for growth

Let us look again at the five dimensions of strategic direction, as shown in Figure 4.1, and then the issues raised in Figure 4.2. This exercise can help to determine whether and how the company should grow.

Organic growth

Organic growth is growth within existing lines of business or existing country markets (or both), or by adding new lines of business or new markets, all within the structure of the current organization. New business

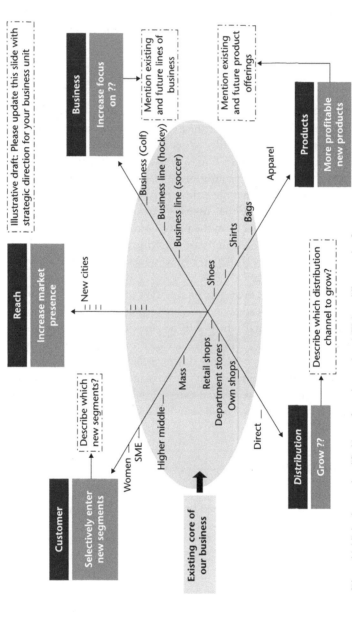

FIGURE 4.1 Proposed strategic direction

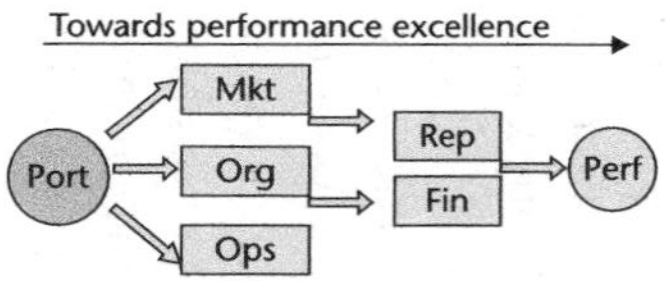

Illustrative: Please update this slide with strategic priorities for your business unit

Strategic priorities

- Double digit organic growth
- Active portfolio management (M&A), including better allocation of capital *(please complete table below)*
- More and stronger partnerships *(please list names)*

Inorganic growth

Current and/or potential M&A deals/strategic partnerships	Strategic rationale	Estimated cost (€mn)	Estimated timing	Expected profit impact (€mn)

Portfolio excellence

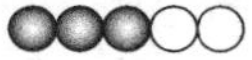

FIGURE 4.2 Portfolio sub-drivers

units are created within the company, rather than being brought in from outside. Some companies prefer organic growth, seeing it as less risky than M&As or partnerships, where cultural clashes can impede the smooth running of the business. With organic growth, the company already knows what it does well and simply carries on doing it. Against this, organic growth can be slower than other forms of growth, and is perceived as being more costly, though there is some evidence that this may not always be so.[2]

If we refer again to Figure 4.1, we can see that organic growth can be achieved along all five dimensions. It can open up new geographical markets, like entering China; or if the company is also operating in China in ten cities, it can decide to accelerate growth by opening in another twenty cities. It can also decide to add other business lines, as in the example of a large car manufacturer deciding to expand in Brazil from private cars into building trucks; or Tata Motors in India, which went the other way, from building trucks to making private cars. All of these choices will require the company to leverage its core capabilities, including distribution channels, managerial and operational skills, and the corporate brand.

Mergers and acquisitions

This term refers to the takeover of other companies and enfolding them into the acquiring company. There is some dispute as to what exactly constitutes a merger and how it differs from an acquisition. An acquisition usually refers to a straightforward takeover of one company by another, usually by a larger (or at least stronger) company of a smaller; though as in the case of Royal Bank of Scotland and NatWest Bank in the UK, or Tata Steel of India and British steelmaker Corus, this is not always so. A merger is supposed to be the coming together of two equals, but as studies have shown, there is nearly always one dominant partner, as in the case of the merger of Thomson International and Reuters in 2008.

We read almost daily in the press about acquisitions that fail to deliver the expected synergies, revenue growth or cost reduction. Between 65 per cent and 80 per cent of M&As fail to deliver the value expected, according to various studies over the years.[3] It is clear that most managers do not pay enough attention to the portfolio driver. They overestimate the benefits, meaning that they pay too much for the real value they are acquiring, and they consistently underestimate the cultural issues involved in making M&As work. Most research shows that most acquisitions are a good deal for the seller but less so for the buyer. The acquisition of ABN

AMRO by RBS in 2007 is a good example of how expected value fails to materialize. On the other hand, there are companies such as GE which manage the process very well. GE generates billions of dollars in profits year on year by actively managing its portfolio of businesses. It creates or acquires businesses and business units in order to grow its portfolio, and then sells these businesses and business units if they have 'matured' or if they better fit in the portfolio of another company.

And the question also has to be asked, and answered, as to whether M&A is the right way forward. If a company lacks certain capabilities within a particular line of business or geography, it then faces the strategic choice of whether to build these capabilities organically or to acquire them. Acquisition is often seen as the quick and easy way to acquire capabilities, but it is also more risky. When Time Warner wanted to get a stake in the booming Internet market, it had two options: build an Internet business from scratch, or acquire an existing player complete with established market presence and skilled staff. Time Warner decided to do the latter and merged with AOL. The deal cost AOL, the acquiring company, $164 billion. But the deal went badly wrong. Cultural incompatibility and communications breakdowns led to the combined Time Warner–AOL posting an annual loss of $100 billion in 2002, a record in US history. This is an exceptional case, but as we noted above, most M&As do not deliver the value that was expected of them, and many fail catastrophically.

One problem, on which researchers have frequently commented, is that M&A decisions were and in some cases still are made on purely financial criteria. If the numbers stack up, then this must be a good deal. The decision-making process ignored issues such as corporate culture and values, which often collide once the merger/acquisition process begins. R. Mukundan, managing director of Tata Chemicals, takes the opposite view; when looking at potential acquisitions, he looks first at their values and checks whether these are in alignment with the values of his own company. If they are, then he feels it is safe to proceed.[4] This point has been made above, but it is repeated here to remind readers of the importance of aligning *all* of the dots. It is not just financial criteria that matter; everything has to line up together if the merger is to succeed.

Partnerships

Partnerships, joint ventures and agencies are all ways of growing a business which can be very useful in certain markets. In some cases, local regulations may require partnerships or joint ventures with local companies, even if this is not the tactically preferrable option. Starbucks has long sought entry to the Indian market, but it stalled when the Indian government demanded the international coffee house chain form a joint venture with an Indian company. Starbucks has never engaged in joint ventures, preferring to wholly own its national subsidiaries, and it refused to change its policy. The impasse prevailed until early 2011 when Starbucks finally found an Indian partner with which it was prepared to work, and compromised on its own policy. Starbucks is finally set to enter the Indian market. In China too, especially the heavily regulated financial sector, such regulations determine the way businesses can operate and compete.

Partnerships and joint ventures are not without their risks, and there are as many stories of failure as of success. The recent business history of China and India is littered with the wreckage of companies that entered incautiously into ventures with the wrong partner, and failed, sometimes catastrophically so. Issues of trust and reliability, of cultural clashes and of local politics benefiting the local partner, can all cause problems that impede the smooth running of a partnership.

Fix it or exit

Finally, in setting and executing the strategy, it is of key importance that managers consider whether they can achieve their performance targets by also identifying business units in the company which are underperforming, or which are simply not fully supporting the organizational strategy and taking up too much management time and attention. From looking at the wide range of data and information that the framework provides, managers can make decisions as to whether these business units should be reorganized and restructured, downsized, or disposed of. Here we can see another link between portfolio drivers and financial drivers (see Chapter 9). One of the important financial drivers is the management of economic value added, a strategic financial management tool which determines whether a business unit or an activity is yielding enough to meet a certain hurdle rate of cost of capital (for example, net 14 per cent per annum). If this is not the case, the result could be that the managers responsible for that business unit are asked to 'fix it or exit', to overhaul the business unit and ensure it becomes more profitable, or to dispose of it.

Some business units may perform functions that can be *outsourced* more cheaply. Others may conduct non-core activities and, if performing well, might represent revenue generating activities. Of course, other issues than just revenue have to be taken into account. For example, what impact will closures or disposals have on staff morale? What impact will they have on the perceptions of stakeholders and consequently on the company's reputation?

Conclusion

When designing and implementing a strategy, most companies do not think explicitly about the portfolio driver. But as we have discussed in this chapter, it is vital to consider the various strategic options for portfolio growth, or even whether growth is desirable and whether some business units might need to be closed or disposed of. Only once the questions about growth have been asked and answered can the right strategic direction be determined.

But the relationship is not all one-way. The strategy of the business itself is modified and changed according to circumstances as time goes on. Nor can strategy be made in a vacuum; strategy makers must take into account the capabilities and situation of the rest of the firm. In succeeding chapters, we will look at how the other parts of the firm fit into the broader strategic picture. In particular, marketing issues have a great deal of impact on strategy, and it is to these that we turn our attention now.

5

THE MARKETING DRIVER

In this chapter we start by defining what marketing excellence means and what it consists of. For our purposes, the key elements of marketing are (1) customer focus, (2) products and services, and (3) sales and distribution. Each of these can then be further broken down into more fine-grained dimensions. For example, customers can be defined in terms of particular customer segments depending on demographics or value focus. In each case once the three key marketing driver elements have been defined by the company, clear objectives and numbers are then added in order to provide information that feeds into the overall planning process.

BOX 5.1 MARKETING DRIVER

1   Customers
2   Products and services
3   Sales and distribution

Figure 5.1 shows the position of the marketing driver related to the other drivers. Figure 5.2 gives an illustrative example of how overall marketing priorities could be set out.

Portfolio	Marketing	Organizational
1. Double digit organic growth 2. Active portfolio management (M&A), including better allocation of capital 3. More and stronger partnerships	4. Introduce profitable new product offerings 5. Increase profitable multi-channel sales 6. Develop strategy for youngsters and women 7. Strengthen customer satisfaction	8. Expand organisational capabilities, including management development 9. Improve performance culture
Operational	**Reputation**	**Financial**
10. Increase efficiency and distributor/customer satisfaction 11. Improve operational risk management 12. Obtain/maintain satisfactory audit rating	13. Increase brand recognition 14. Strengthen compliance 15. Communicate clearly to internal/external stakeholders 16. Ensure integrity, ethical behaviour in all areas	17. Raise $ capital + debt 18. Expand value-based management 19. Strengthen risk mgt 20. Improve MIS & control

FIGURE 5.1 Strategic priorities

Figure 5.2 is an example of a template developed at ING. As noted in the small print at the bottom of the template, managers should consider the interdependencies between customer segments, sales channels and products, rather than simply looking at each element in isolation. Some products are easy to sell through a variety of channels. Others, like iTunes, e-books or e-tickets, can only be sold through one channel, the Internet. Customers also have their own ideas about the channels they would like to use. When purchasing a car, for instance, customers might prefer to 'experience' the car in a showroom rather than online.

These three sub-drivers are then cascaded down into other lower level sub-drivers. Issues such as pricing, point of sale (location), communications (advertising), customer support and the like all form part of the marketing driver. Readers by now will remember that the most important requirement of any management framework should be that the design and connectivity of all drivers and sub-drivers follows the 3Cs principle; that is, they must be consistent, complete and comprehensive. How often do we find companies that claim they are creating 'customer delight', when in fact customers are experiencing increasing frustration as they try to order products or get through to malfunctioning call centres? In order to 'be 3C', there must be alignment not only within the marketing driver but also between the marketing driver and other drivers.

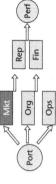

Towards performance excellence

Illustrative: Please update this slide with strategic priorities for your business unit

Strategic priorities
- Introduce profitable new product offerings
- Increase profitable multi-channel sales
- Develop strategy for youngsters and women segmentation
- Strengthen customer satisfaction

Please note that marketing is the sum of customer segments, products and distribution channels, including their interdependencies. In this section, you should be consistent with the strategic direction as captured in the Spider slide. If that is self explanatory, reference can be made to these slides and no further explanation is needed.

Marketing excellence

FIGURE 5.2 Marketing

Take for example the issue of marketing reach, in other words, the locations and where the company will seek customers and market its products and services (see Figure 5.2). The framework requires that locations where the company intends to expand be listed and ranked specifically. Yet this issue is also covered by the portfolio driver; as we saw in Chapter 4, this driver also requires managers to list any regions into which expansion is considered. Now suppose that under the portfolio driver no expansion was considered necessary, yet here under the marketing driver managers are clearly considering expansion! This would indicate a clash of interests, one not necessarily good for the entire company. Aligning the drivers in this way forces managers to engage in 'joined-up thinking' and see the whole picture.

Or let us take another example and look at issues such as advertising and branding. These are of course core aspects of marketing (even if many companies are organized so that branding activities are carried out by corporate communications rather than the marketing department *per se*). But branding does more than just build brand equity; it also helps to grow the company's overall reputation. We go on to discuss branding in more detail in Chapter 8 as well as considering it in this chapter, for the simple reason that branding is important in both cases. Again, joined-up thinking is required.

The importance of getting marketing aligned with the other drivers cannot be overstated. Marketing plays an essential role in enabling businesses to achieve their goals. Although managers sometimes forget this, businesses depend absolutely on their customers. As Peter Drucker once wrote, 'the only valid purpose of a business is to create a customer'.[1]

BOX 5.2 CONNECTING THE DOTS . . .

How marketing drivers impact on other drivers

Portfolio drivers: It is easy for a strategist to establish a goal such as achieving market leadership in a certain sector, or to target a new market for entry. But this goal will never be achieved if there are not sufficient customers with enough spending power and the will to buy the company's products and services. Data from marketing will – or should – impact directly on strategic thinking. The choice of portfolio has to be a realistic one, reflecting the company's ability to reach and serve customers in a profitable way.

Organizational drivers: The organizational form that a company takes will be determined in part by the company's customers, their location, the nature of the distribution channel and the nature of the product. An Internet retailer, whose customers are distributed over a wide geographical area and served remotely, will require a different organizational set-up from a hotel chain or a restaurant where there is a high degree of customer contact. Similarly, there will be different HR requirements between, say, a software consultancy and a mining company. Different skill levels and different levels of motivation will be reflected in differences in management style, and also in compensation.

Operational drivers: Imagine how much 3C alignment is needed to produce, sell and deliver 37 million iPhones, as was done by Apple in the fourth quarter in 2011. Think about the extremely efficient (global) processes needed in the sourcing of material, production, logistics, after sales, etc., to ensure that marketing can deliver the 'customer delight' as envisioned by the company. Thus operations and marketing have to work closely together. The first makes the products, the other sells them. History is full of technically perfect products that failed because they did not match customer needs. Marketing has a responsibility to tell operations what customers want; operations has a responsibility to listen and then take appropriate action. But marketing should also consider what the potential and the constraints of operations are.

Reputational drivers: A brand can be defined as the sum total of customers' perceptions of the company and its products. Brands can be very valuable and very powerful, but they can also be easily destroyed. The quality of a company's products and services, the behaviour and demeanour and even appearance of its sales staff all impact on brand and reputation. People judge a company by what they see and hear, as well as its products themselves. If a restaurant's staff are rude and aggressive, then no matter how good the food it is unlikely that we will ever eat there again. If sales staff use 'hard sell' techniques that break financial services laws or regulations, then this too will impact on the overall reputation.

Financial drivers: As noted, selling products to customers provides the source of the company's revenue stream and hence (might) generate profits, and further, customer attitudes to the brand help generate brand equity. It follows that how well marketing performs its tasks will impact on the company in terms of revenue, profits and brand value. But whether that indeed will be or is the case, financial analysis, control and accounting are needed. The finance department requires timely and accurate data, including forecast data, from the marketing department in order to estimate current and future revenues; sound financial planning and determining whether certain activities are contributing to the prosperity of the company and its stakeholders is almost impossible otherwise.

Customers provide the revenue streams and profits that enable the business to grow and expand. Although revenues can be boosted in the short term through takeovers, over the long run unless customers continue to buy the company's products and services, these gains will prove illusory.

Yet marketing does not always receive the important place it deserves in strategic thinking. As long ago as 1960, Theodore Levitt remarked in his famous article 'Marketing Myopia' that too many companies are led by production and innovation concerns, rather than by the realities of the market:

> Another big danger to a firm's continued growth arises when top management is wholly transfixed by the profit possibilities of technical research and development . . . What gets shortchanged are the realities of the *market* . . . The emphasis on production becomes particularly attractive when the product can be made at declining unit costs. There is no more inviting way of making money than by running the plant full blast.[2]

In a similar vein, Tim Ambler in his book *Marketing Metrics* warns that many companies are still focused on bottom line growth and pay too little attention to where that growth actually comes from. 'Accountants seem to imagine that a pile of money will grow if only you count it often enough', is his comment.[3] Ambler believes that part of the fault also lies with marketing departments, which too often exist in silos of their own and seem to play by different rules from the rest of the business. He urges strongly that marketing departments need to become more rigorous, pay more attention to hard metrics and become better at sharing information and integrating with the rest of the business.

There is more to the marketing drivers than just pleasing customers, of course. As the marketing literature tells us, firms need first to determine who their customers are and what their needs are, then work out how to provide products and services at a price which ensures a reasonable profit for the company itself, then to make customers aware of the product or service offering and finally to determine how and where the exchange between customers will take place: the famous four Ps of product, place, price and promotion.[4] Doing this successfully brings direct benefits in terms of building streams and generating profits as noted above, but also indirect benefits in the form of 'brand equity', the value of the company's product brands and its corporate brand.[5] There are a number of different ways of calculating brand equity, but all of them include estimates of customer feeling for the brand and customer satisfaction as key components.

Customers

Although the shelves of business books in most bookstores are stacked with books such as Kim and Mauborgne's *Blue Ocean Strategy*, urging managers to think boldly and make breakthough innovations that will take them beyond the competition, there is another strand of thinking that offers another point of view.[6] Books such as Barwise and Meehan's *Beyond the Familiar* or Collins and Hansen's *Great By Choice* suggest that firms that are successful over the long term – in Collins and Hansen's study, this means outperforming the index for their industry by a factor of 10 or more over 40 years – do so by sticking very close to their customers and providing what they want, day in and day out, year in and year out. Examples include Apple, Intel, Microsoft and Procter & Gamble. These are highly innovative firms, but most if not all of their innovations are small, incremental and customer-led in nature; improving existing products and services a bit at a time rather than constantly introducing things that are revolutionary and new.

Clearly, then, companies and managers have many options to choose from in determining their marketing strategy and how they will achieve growth by serving customers. But one thing is common across all these different approaches: the customer must be served, and served well. Failing to meet customer needs is not an option if the company wishes to succeed. In these highly competitive times, there are always plenty of rivals waiting to step in and take over a company's customers should it fail to satisfy their need and wants. And meeting their needs means – to repeat – determining who customers are, creating and selling products that they want, building distribution channels that do so swiftly and efficiently, and building strong brands; and doing so in a way that meets the requirements of the three Cs: consistency, completeness and comprehensiveness.

Once again, we need to begin by looking at the options for strategic direction. This chart (Figure 5.3) is intended to guide *strategic* thinking, but the relevance to marketing is obvious. Line of business, customers, products, distribution channels, reach: these are all issues that marketing departments deal with every day. This connection means that it stands to reason that the rest of the business must take account of these drivers too. And here also is an important reason for not letting the marketing department drift off to become a silo of its own. If we accept the notion that customers are necessary for long-term growth, then it must be seen at once that the marketing department plays an absolutely vital role, for it is the primary interface between the company and its customers. That means that the whole company, not just the marketing department, has a stake in success and as some have argued in the past, the whole company, not just the marketing department, should be behind the marketing effort. The French president Clémenceau once remarked that war is too important a matter to be left to generals. By the same token, we can observe that marketing is too important to be left only to the marketing department. Everyone in the company, directly or indirectly, needs to be involved even if they never actually see or speak to a customer. That means, as we discussed in Chapter 1, that there must be a focus on connecting all the organizational 'dots' and bringing the whole organization to focus on creating customer satisfaction. There is no one thing that is 'most important'. Instead it is the total process with everyone and everything equally involved, that leads to performance excellence.

The marketing dimension

All managers across the company need to be able to ask, and have answered, the following questions:

1. What customers are we serving? What are their characteristics, their wants and needs?
2. What products and services do we make and sell, and what do customers think of these?
3. How do we reach customers in order to make the sale and deliver products and services?

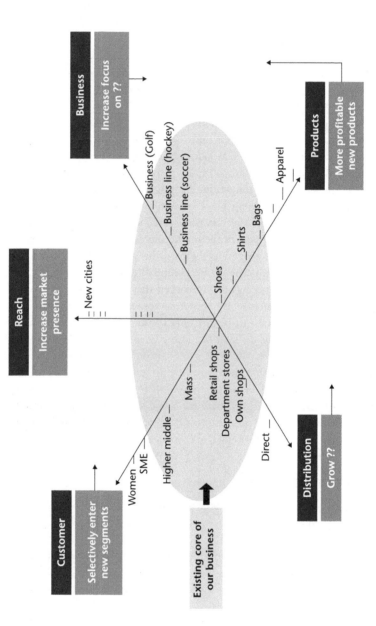

FIGURE 5.3 Proposed strategic direction

There are no template answers to these questions, for the answer will vary from company to company and even from business unit to business unit, or geography to geography, within the company. Different customers in different countries perceive brands in entirely different ways. Smirnoff vodka is regarded as a 'premium' brand in Canada and commands a higher price than in America, where it is seen as a 'bar' brand. Toyota's luxury car brand Lexus is perceived very differently in Europe than in America, where it is highly popular. The shape and nature of the distribution channel will depend on the country, its geography, existing infrastructure systems, existing retail systems, the nature of the product or service, the location of customers and many other factors.

It is highly important that these questions be asked and answered – whatever the answers might be. It is also important to keep asking the questions, over and over again. It is inevitable that the answers to these questions will change over time. Customer needs change as people move locations, grow older, become more or less affluent. New technologies invade the market and render existing products obsolete, as happened famously when digital cameras arrived on the scene and knocked out the market for camera film. Earlier we mentioned that it is important for frameworks to be flexible in order to accommodate changing situations. Here is a case in point. By providing accurate and timely information, the framework allows managers to spot changes in the market early and move to take appropriate action.

Many companies use marketing tools to gather such information. These tools range from simple market research to sophisticated customer relationship management (CRM) systems. However, the purpose of most of these is merely to disseminate information inside the marketing department. We argue that this is not good enough. Changes in the market require a response not just from the marketing department but from operations and production, procurement, finance and other functions too.

Marketing information must be incorporated into the overarching management framework. All relevant data are 'uploaded' by all relevant stakeholders in the organization and accessible by all. Without this information, managers in other areas of the business do not have the necessary information to make sound business decisions.

When considering the question 'what customers are we serving?', the usual first distinction is between individual customers, or retail customers, and businesses or other institutions (see Figure 5.4). Each has

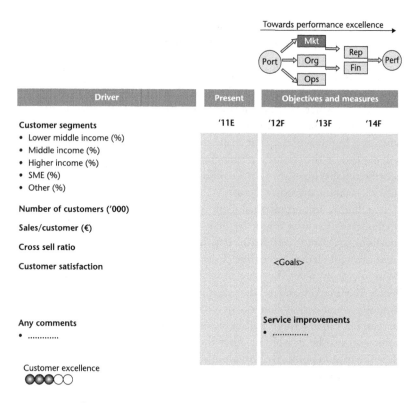

FIGURE 5.4 Customer segments

quite distinctive characteristics, including different needs and different levels of buying power. There are some hybrids that serve both at once: for example, 'DIY' retail operations sell to both householders looking for materials and tools to improve their homes, and plumbers, electricians, builders and other small businesses engaged in home building and repair. Again, it is important for the company to very clear what its customer base is.

In terms of retail customers, the information that a company needs to collect can be broken down into three separate categories: *demographic*, *socio-cultural* and *psychographic*. Each of these categories contains important levels of information about customers. Of course most companies will serve people with many different characteristics, and one important process is to group together those customers with similar characteristics, a process that marketers refer to as 'segmentation'.

Demographic information includes factors such as age, gender, race, nationality, family status (married, with children, etc.), work status (including such categories as self-employed and retired), educational background, personal income and so on. Demographic information tells us what customers' backgrounds are and gives us clues as to what their needs are likely to be and what buying power they have at their disposal. The ABC classification is one way of categorizing people by demographic background.

Socio-cultural information includes factors such as national regional culture and its influences including language, religion, traditions, customs and superstitions. Socio-cultural information helps managers to understand what the eminent scholar of business culture Geert Hofstede referred to as 'software of the mind'.[7] It sheds light on personal beliefs and motivation which can affect buying decisions and patterns.

Psychographic information describes personal beliefs and values and helps managers to attempt to understand personal motivation. There are various means of classifying psychographic data, the earliest and still most widely used being Maslow's hierarchy of needs.[8] According to Maslow, people start off by trying to satisfy basic needs such as those for food, shelter and safety, and once these are established they then move on to higher needs such as self-esteem and the need to belong to a group. Others have adapted the hierarchy of needs to different markets; for example, Rama Bijapurkar classified Indian consumers in ascending order as the resigned, the strivers, the mainstreamers, the aspirers and the successful.[9]

Put together, these three classes of data help to define the company's customers in terms of their needs and values and thus assist managers to better understand whom they are dealing with. Properly used, these data should then help managers to develop products and services closely aligned to the needs of the different target segments.

Business to business customers

Here the list of customer characteristics is simpler and includes factors such as the size of the customer business, its buying power and credit rating, its reputation for prompt payment, its location and even its own viability as a business. Given the time and effort that have to be put into building relationships with B2B customers, it is useful to know if they are likely to stay in business. Because B2B customers tend to be high value in terms of revenue and profits, losing one can be painful in financial terms.

Marketing's interface role

As noted above, marketing is the primary interface between the company and its customers. Through marketing come data and information from a key external stakeholder group. In effect, the marketing function offers a kind of 'window on the world' to the rest of the company.

Hence the absolute importance of this particular marketing driver to the framework. Without knowledge about customers, the company is effectively operating in the dark. Thus, data and information about customers must be widely and readily available throughout the framework. Equally important is the need for this information to be updated, as often as possible. Because customers change and their needs change, the company must be always ready to adapt its customer response.

Products

The template shown in Figure 5.5 is an example of how to capture information (objectives, numbers and so on) about which product ranges exist already and which products need to be added or improved. It can be as detailed and specific as people think is required for the coming planning process. If it has been decided that the product manual should be improved or the material of the packaging should be more environmentally friendly to meet the new corporate responsibility policy, then this information should be listed here. Such information is amongst other things relevant for the operation/production departments that make the products, as well as for the people involved in improving the company's reputation through better corporate responsibility.

When we talk of 'products', we are of course talking about services as well. Services are different from products in several ways. Most importantly, products are purchased by the customer and then taken away to be consumed at a later date, while most services (hotel accommodation, medical care) are consumed at the moment of purchase. Of course many 'products' are a hybrid of product and service. A customer's satisfaction from a restaurant meal depends partly on the service provided by the waiter but also partly on the quality of the food, the 'product'.[10] Customer satisfaction derived from the purchase of a car may be as much to do with the warranty and after sales service as with the car itself. Marketers have come up with the term 'bundle of benefits' to describe all the various product and service benefits that the customer derives from a purchase.

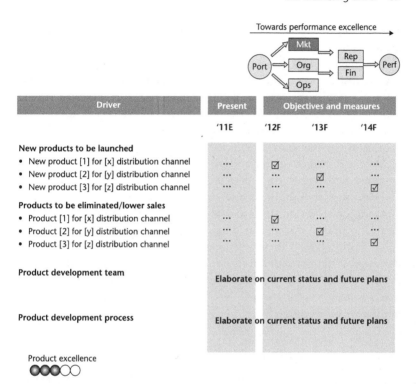

FIGURE 5.5 Product

Product drivers deal with product features included in the bundle of benefits. They tell us what the product can do, or is designed to do. They can be seen as a specification of product features, but should also include information on conceivable product uses. This information can then be matched to customer needs as determined above, to find out whether the product and its bundle of benefits really do match customer needs. One common problem is building products which the company thinks are wonderful but which customers reject. We think of Apple today as a company that produces easy-to-use products that deliver a lot of satisfaction, but some of Apple's earlier products were over-engineered and too complex. When Nokia took the lead in the mobile phone market from Motorola by moving into digital technology, Motorola's engineers responded with a very sophisticated mobile phone design. But the new Motorola phone didn't do what customers wanted, and the product failed to make an impact on Nokia's commanding share of the market.[11]

Important here is the measurement of product quality. Quality is generally defined as 'fitness' for use; that is, does the product deliver the value that the customer expects of it? If it does, then it is considered to be of good quality. The Fiat Panda and the Rolls-Royce are both considered to be quality cars because they deliver on customer expectations, even though they are at opposite ends of the price and build range.

Most companies attempt to assess product quality by measuring customer satisfaction. In *Beyond the Familiar*, Patrick Barwise and Seán Meehan urge companies to also measure customer *dissatisfaction*. How many customers are unhappy, and why? They cite the example of one B2B services company that measured customer satisfaction and thought it had good relationships with its customers. When the company introduced measures of customer dissatisfaction, however, it found that there were many hitherto concealed problems and relationships were nowhere near as strong as managers had thought. This enabled corrective action to be taken to improve relationships.[12]

Sales and distribution

Again, Figure 5.6 is an example of how a sales and distribution template might look. Each company or business unit can design and adapt such templates to meet their own needs, depending on what line of business they are in. The framework should here capture 3C information about how to use the sales/distribution driver to offer products to selected customer segments according to the overall business plan. There should also be an overview of how sales revenue will be spread over the various channels, split by product. Such breakdowns can also be done by customer group. This information can be helpful in, for example, setting sales targets and determining end-of-year bonus settings.

Competitive value proposition

How do we know that our product value proposition is really competitive? When this question is being discussed, managers tend to selectively highlight just a couple of aspects to make their point as to why their product is competitive. They may use statements such as 'our product is the best buy in town'. Yet is the price, given a certain level of quality, the only feature

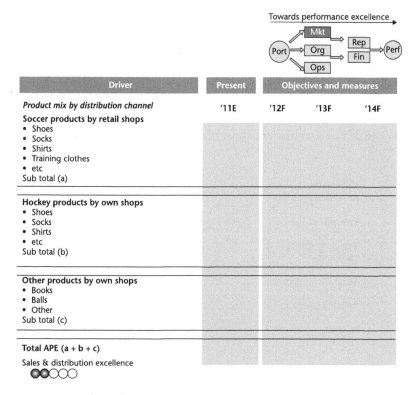

FIGURE 5.6   Sales and distribution

that is relevant? What about issues such as brand, service, options, easiness to acquire and use, warranties and so on? Therefore smart managers study and consider constantly all the features that matter to the customer, including those that matter today as well as tomorrow. Traditionally the strategic goal is to beat your competitor. The trouble is, if your competitor is doing the same, you will end up in a 'bloody, red ocean', at least according to W. Chan Kim and Renée Mauborgne in their book *Blue Ocean Strategy*.[13] When designing a strategy based on big ideas and mapping all the features of your own and your competitors' products, you can see more profoundly and clearly which of your own product/service features really make a difference, and use this to help create a 'blue ocean' strategy. Chan and Mauborgne introduced a simple tool to map the differences on all the features relevant to the targeted customer, onto a *canvas*. A similar approach was proposed by David J. Collins and Michael G. Rustad in *Harvard*

Business Review in 2008, when they compared Wal-Mart's value proposition with that of Sears and local 'mom and pop' retailers (Figure 5.7).[14]

The sales and distribution channels that the company uses to make customers aware of its products and then deliver to them will differ of course, depending on the nature of the product and the nature of the customer. Increasingly, companies are using multiple channels. Large multiple grocery retailers increasingly use both stores and Internet shopping to deliver to customers, aware that that they have one market segment

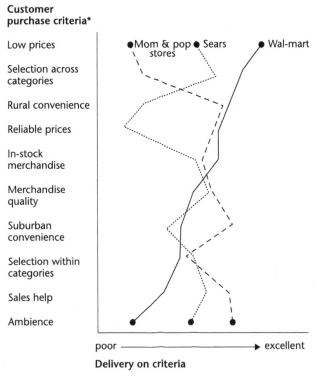

FIGURE 5.7   Wal-Mart's value proposition

Source: Collis, David J. and Rukstad, Michael G. (2008) 'Can You Say What Your Strategy Is?', *Harvard Business Review*, 7(4): 1–10.

that prefers to shop in person and another that prefers the convenience of the Internet – and a third segment that switches from one mode to the other from time to time, depending on their own circumstances. For example, a busy working mother may find it convenient to order groceries over the Internet one day, but later might find it equally convenient to pop into the store while on her way home from work.

The company should use information from marketing drivers to audit its sales and distribution channels and determine their fitness for purpose. First, how does the company reach its customers with information about products? How does it communicate, either through above-the-line methods (primarily advertising) or below-the-line methods such as promotions and public relations? How effective are these communications, and what impact do they have on the company's reputation more generally (see Chapter 8)? Are the company's communications targeted at meeting customer needs?

In terms of physical distribution, the key metrics are timeliness – is the product available when the customer wants it? – and reliability – is the product available where the customer wants it? These cannot be overlooked. One common mistake in the early days by Internet retailers was to assume that the most important point of the exchange was the transaction on the Internet. This was not always so. Products such as clothes, books and food still had to be physically transported to the customer. Failure to deliver in a timely fashion cost many of these retailers dearly in terms of revenue and reputation as customers turned elsewhere to look for more reliable sellers.

Brand equity

Brand equity is the monetary value of a brand, which can be listed on a balance sheet as one of the company's assets. Brand equity is a controversial subject, not least because the leading brand valuation agencies such as Brand Finance and Interbrand measure value in different ways and reach different valuation figures. In 2007 one valuation agency measured the value of the Coca-Cola brand at $43 billion while another valued it at $67 billion. Early calculations of brand value used crude measures such as estimating value at equivalent to a year's turnover for the brand. Today, a commonly used method is to arrive at a net earnings figure, which is brand revenues minus operating costs, taxes and a charge for the use of capital. A brand discount rate is then applied, reflecting the brand's positioning relevant to its key competitors, likely volatility in key markets and overall reputation with stakeholder groups including customers and employees.

Whatever method is used, and whatever value is arrived it, it is safe to say that all companies, big and small, have a brand equity, a combination of their brand's revenue-generating capacity and its reputation (and the two are of course closely linked, as obviously brands with good reputations will usually generate more revenue than will competing brands with bad reputations). This means that companies need to monitor their brands, and information about brand and reputation need to be communicated and updated regularly. As Mary Jo Hatch and Majken Schultz have pointed out, the attitudes of employees also have a powerful influence on brand value.[15] Employees are also often customers; and they can also communicate their views about the company and its brand through a variety of channels. We will come on to this point in more detail in Chapter 6.

Marketing drivers and the organizational framework

Most large companies will have a department in charge of marketing and some will have subordinate teams in charge of products and managing sales or distribution channels. Rarely will a company have a 'customer department' as such. They might have a customer support centre, but this will be typically part of the operations department. The choices to be made for setting the strategic priorities for the marketing sub-drivers (customers, products, sales/distribution) will be made by senior business unit managers along with the respective functional managers. When all of these managers have access to the same templates with a full set of 3C data, decision-making should become faster and more effective. (In Chapter 6 we will look at this issue again under the heading of the organizational driver, where we will discuss how *responsibility and accountability* within the organizational matrix can be created.)

Adaptability and flexibility

Every business today operates in a dynamic world where change is constant. Marketing is as much affected by this as any other part of the business, perhaps more. Customer preferences change rapidly, calling for new products and different marketing strategies. How can the company be sure that its frameworks will enable and support change, rather than becoming a rigid constraint that hinders adaptability and flexibility?

To answer the question, let us take as analogy a person travelling around Paris. If he has no road map or GPS, then he will struggle to find his way. But he if does have a detailed, 3C map of the city or a functioning and up-to-date GPS, then he should be able to navigate without difficulty. It is the same when running a business in a constantly changing environment. The management framework provides the roadmap – usually in the form of a business plan, though it must be an adaptable and flexible one. This helps managers to know where they are meant to go (into which new markets, which new products need to be developed, and so on). Adaptation is a matter of picking up the relevant templates and updating them to take account of new and changing circumstances, thus in effect deciding on a change of route on the map. Other people can then be informed about these changes, and sign off when needed, in a very efficient and effective way.

And in fact, this is quite different from how most managers are now struggling to deal with change within their companies. Most are operating in silos without properly engaging and informing other relevant stakeholders. They drive through Paris without a roadmap. They often use plans which are incomplete, out of date, incomprehensive and inconsistent, causing them to soon lose their way. Far from being rigid, then, the framework should become an adaptive, enabling device which helps to keep managers focused on the thing that matters most: creating value for customers, yet in a constant adaptive way.

Conclusion

Ask ten managers what is meant by 'marketing' and you will get ten different answers. Some will say it means sales, others will refer to branding and advertising and so on. The first important step, then, is to define what is meant by 'marketing', what the term encompasses. This done, managers can begin sharing the information needed to develop and execute the overall strategy. Information is captured under the headings of customers, products and sales/distribution, which will cascade down using the various levels of the organization. As we noted above, it is important to ensure the interdependencies are well understood and managed.

Other departments will use marketing information when setting and managing their own drivers. The need for adaptability and flexibility is not only crucial in the marketing function, but in all other drivers as well.

Of course, how well the company responds will depend, among other things, on whether it has the organizational capability to do so. It is to this organizational driver that we shall turn our attention in the next chapter.

6

THE ORGANIZATIONAL DRIVER

As well as setting out the strategy and its priorities (asking 'what' questions) and the execution (asking 'how' questions), the company must also ask and answer the 'who' questions. Who will be responsible for executing which parts of the strategy? Many companies struggle with this. Staff and managers are unsure as to their own role and responsibilities within the company. Mostly this is because the business processes themselves are unclear and not 3C (not consistent, complete or comprehensive), and therefore people do not really know what is expected of them. Bad management practices can also lead to tensions between line and function, or between head office and the regions. These too can create uncertainties, situations where people are not sure what they are responsible for, or to whom. Issues such as management development, training, career development, compensation and so on are also an important part of the organizational driver for performance excellence.

The main organizational 'dots' to be connected are listed in Box 6.1.

BOX 6.1 ORGANIZATIONAL DRIVERS

- Organizational setting
- Human resources management
- Compensation

Portfolio	Marketing	Organizational
1. Double digit organic growth 2. Active portfolio management (M&A), including better allocation of capital 3. More and stronger partnerships	4. Introduce profitable new product offerings 5. Increase profitable multi-channel sales 6. Develop strategy for youngsters and women 7. Strengthen customer satisfaction	8. Expand organisational capabilities, including management development 9. Improve performance culture
Operational	**Reputation**	**Financial**
10. Increase efficiency and distributor/customer satisfaction 11. Improve operational risk management 12. Obtain/maintain satisfactory audit rating	13. Increase brand recognition 14. Strengthen compliance 15. Communicate clearly to internal/external stakeholders 16. Ensure integrity, ethical behaviour in all areas	17. Raise $ capital + debt 18. Expand value-based management 19. Strengthen risk mgt 20. Improve MIS & control

FIGURE 6.1 Strategic priorities

Figures 6.1 and 6.2 show an example of a statement of strategic priorities for the organizational driver. This may look like a high-level approach, and it is. It is important to start from the top and work down, setting out clearly formulated and framed organizational priorities which recognize what works (and what does not) across the entire organization. For example, we might state that we want to *improve organizational (and personal) capabilities*, because many other activities such as training, motivation, culture, compensation, hiring and firing will support this overriding objective. Management can also set a strategic goal to *improve the performance culture* to help strengthen the company's competitive position and push for better results (more sales, less cost, higher profits, more value). Or it could decide that the *ethical standards, values and awareness* should be enhanced to protect the company from (further) reputational damage and to improve the company's reputation and competitive position. Thereafter further and more detailed actions and goals will be set out in subsequent, more detailed templates.

Structure and people

Organizations are essential for getting things done, in business as in all walks of life. Throughout the history of human civilization there has been

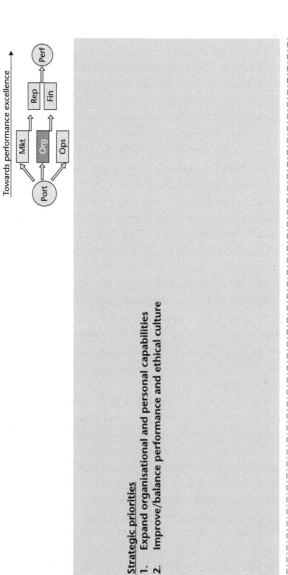

Towards performance excellence

Port → Mkt / Org / Ops → Rep / Fin → Perf

Strategic priorities

1. **Expand organisational and personal capabilities**
2. **Improve/balance performance and ethical culture**

Key HR themes are:
- Building organisational capabilities to outperform competition and gain market share
- Management development has been identified as a key strategic priority
- "Structure follows strategy" – organizational structure should be well aligned with corporate strategy

Organizational excellence

FIGURE 6.2   Setting the organizational strategic priorities

a constant struggle to find the best and most effective way or organizing, the best way of harnessing the combined efforts of a group so that they amount to more than just the sum total of the efforts of individuals. Two aspects of organization stand in particular as having a direct effect on the planning and execution of strategy. First, there is the *form* of the organization: the structure that determines how people work together, who is responsible for what and who takes on the ultimate responsibility of leadership. The second aspect is the *people* who make up the organization. Are they aware of the organization's purpose, and do they have the necessary skills to execute plans and help the organization achieve that purpose?

In the world of business, both structure and people are of fundamental importance and both can make or break a business as it tries to achieve its goals. The wrong organizational form can hamper a business badly. In 1982, Tom Peters and Robert Waterman in their book *In Search of Excellence* described how big, vertically structured, hierarchial American companies were failing to meet the challenge posed by their more flexible and agile Japanese rivals.[1] But the problem can go the other way too. Too little control can be as dangerous as too much. The danger of managers or even entire business units going off and doing their own thing, not in line with, or even working actively against, the company's best interests, is always there. The divisive split between the accounting and consulting arms of Arthur Andersen ended ultimately with the consulting arm separating and going its own way, leaving the original accountancy firm to disappear entirely after the scandal of Enron.

Today, many different forms of organization exist in the business world. Still popular is the oldest business model of all, the family: most small and some medium-sized enterprises continue to be organized as family businesses, especially in Asia. Big hierarchical bureaucracies continue to exist in America and Europe. Japanese companies adopted what Nonaka and Takeuchi call the 'o-form' organization, with decentralized business units linked by strong horizontal channels of communication. Large Indian business groups like Tata and Reliance also rely on decentralization with only very light central control.

From this, it will be seen that there is no generic best way of organizing. The organization that works well for a steel mill will not necessarily work for a graphic design agency. A small specialist software consultancy might prefer a very loose organizational form, while a precision engineering company might feel the need for tighter control and better communications in order to ensure quality. It depends partly too on the people involved. Are they highly skilled and highly motivated and willing to take responsibility for their own work? Or do they prefer direction and control from above? Both sorts of people exist, and both will be suited to some kinds of work and not to others. Management frameworks need to be designed to take these variations into account, rather than assuming that all people work and behave in the same ways. Centralized and decentralized organizations both need frameworks; but what those frameworks look like and how they are used will vary.

Different corporate structures to drive different strategies

Most entrepreneurs do start as a single ownership company or as a partnership. These are easy to set up, low cost and simple to manage. Yet when the company starts to expand and needs more capital, a more formal legal corporate structure will be used. More shareholders will be brought in to finance the growth of the company. Some will first try to get funding from friends and family, a way very much followed in financing the growth of the millions of small companies, especially in Asia. The more successful ones will go for the 'private equity' option or sell the company at an early stage to a venture capital fund. While many companies are legally operating in the form of an incorporated company or a publicly listed company, they are certainly not the only option to be considered. Another less used form is the *cooperative*, such as the very successful Rabobank from the Netherlands. Their clients 'own' the local co-op banks, allowing the decision-making process to be very close to where their local customers and 'owners' are. Their central office is 'just' to support the local units, with local authority being above central authority. Another interesting organizational model is the one applied so successfully by John Lewis, Britain's department store of choice, which is basically owned and run by their staff. One reason for this effective model is the well managed combination of participative management style, employee ownership and profit sharing.[2]

Organizational setting

If we accept the point made above, that there is no one best way of organizing a business and the best form of organization will always be dependent on the nature of the business, its customers and the other strategic issues discussed above, then we come to another question: How does the framework enable managers to design the optimal organization that is fit for purpose, and to maintain that optimality by adapting to changing conditions? The organizational 'chapter' of the framework has three key functions in this respect: it defines roles and responsibilities, it establishes channels of reporting and control, and it establishes communications formats to ensure consistency across the firm.

Defining roles and responsibilities

Most businesses will have an organization chart that defines what the official roles and duties of staff and managers are, and most employees will also have these duties enshrined in their own job descriptions. However, these definitions and descriptions are not always well circulated. It is often the case that people know very clearly what their own duties and responsibilities are, but they have no idea of what other people around them are supposed to be doing. This makes it very difficult to achieve coordinated effective action.

Recall that one of the purposes of organization is to ensure that the combined efforts of the group are greater than the sum of the efforts of the individuals. This can be seen very clearly in sport. Take eleven talented individual players and put them on a soccer field without explaining what the game plan is or what each player is meant to do, and they will probably fail. On the other hand, a team of less talented players might succeed if they all know clearly not only their own roles but also those of everyone else on the pitch. This means they can count on other players to be in certain positions at the right time and defend and attack effectively. Coordination of roles is one of the key features of organization. Thus the framework needs to 'connect the dots' and assist people to understand what is going on around them.

Establishing channels of reporting and control

The free flow of accurate and timely information is another of the key tasks of the framework. As we have noted already, many organizations are characterized by silos and solid ceilings which inhibit communication and make it impossible for people to know what is going on in other parts of the business. Studies over the past several decades have shown that when people are starved of information, they lose motivation and become less effective.

Establishing communications formats

One of the consequences of loss of central control and the development of silos is that different business units will develop their own ways of communicating, even their own languages. In his book *Reinventing the CFO*, Jeremy Holt describes how some finance departments produce reports in a language which is very useful to themselves but virtually unintelligible to people in other business functions.[3] This problem occurs especially in finance, but is not unique to it.

Thus another purpose of the framework must be to ensure that there is a single clear and consistent mode of communication across the entire company, which distributes information accurately and in a manner that all staff can understand.

The organization chart

The organization chart should demonstrate clearly who is doing what and what each person's position and role is in the organization. It should be set out using clear and simple terms and graphics. Each business unit present its 'org chart' in the same shape and format and with the same 'language', although the content can – and should – be customized. Figure 6.3 gives an example. The dark blue lines represent the business units, which can be best described as those organizational units or departments which are responsible for a *profit and loss* (P/L) budget. This is contrary to a functional department (like HR) which is responsible for a *cost* budget. Functions gives support to the business units. The sum of the P/Ls of all business units should add up to the company's total budget, since all costs will have to be allocated to the business units *pro rata* their 'take' of the support that the functions provide.

The organizational matrix

Almost every organization operates with various functional departments and several business units. As said, most functional departments, such as finance and HR, give support to more than one business unit. If this is indeed the case, we can call the 'fabric' of the organizational setting a *matrix* organization. As is shown in Figure 6.3, the matrix has the functional (horizontal) lines going across the (vertical) business unit lines. This reflects how certain global functions have a role supporting both the

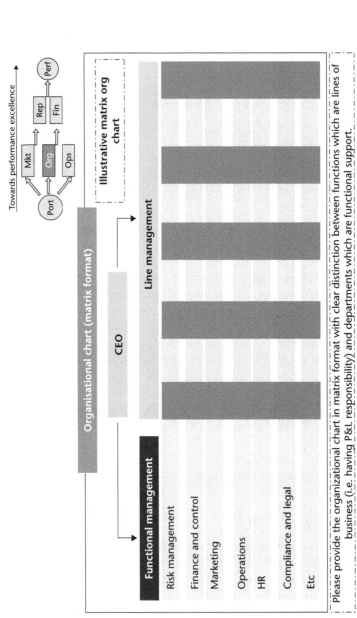

FIGURE 6.3 Organizational setting in the form of a matrix

functional departments and the business line; an example might be Global Customer Support.

One of the complicating issues of a matrix organization is that most people have to report to two heads: to a line manager and at the same time to a functional manager. It is therefore crucial that leaders explain very clearly how a matrix is working. This could be done as follows:

1. Explain clearly that each organization has and needs a matrix. It might be that they present their org chart in the form of a hierarchical chart, but this is a less effective way of showing people what the real organizational setting is. Why? In a hierarchical chart, the organization is shown or 'pictured' in a *one*-dimensional way, with the lines representing who is reporting to whom. Most companies have organized themselves in business units and functional departments. However, in a purely hierarchical org chart people cannot see the distinction between which unit is a business unit and which one is a function. When, for example, it is not clear whether 'sales' is a business unit or a support function, conflict and confusion might arise.

2. Make sure each business unit and function includes the org chart itself in their business plan and presentations. In most strategic plans the org chart is missing, and thus the plan does not address the very important 'who' question. This problem can best be solved by having all business units use the same matrix org chart, so that managers will get complete, consistent and comprehensive (3C) information from each unit about how the 'who' question is organized. In this way all matrix templates can also be 'piled up' and aligned and connected to each other at the different layers of an organization.

3. Explain clearly and in simple words the differences between a business unit (which has a profit/loss responsibility, based on external revenues) and a function (a cost centre with the costs being recharged to other BUs/functions).

4. Make sure that each matrix org chart clearly indicates which reporting line represents a function and which one a business line. People should not be left unclear as to whether they are part of a business unit or of a function.

5. Explain clearly the different roles and responsibilities of line managers and functional managers.

Aligning organization with strategy

There has in the past been considerable debate about the relationship between business strategy and organizational structure. Alfred Chandler, one of the 'founding fathers' of modern business strategy, coined the term 'structure follows strategy' and argued that a firm should first set out its strategy and then determine the best organizational structure that will support the strategy, and then adopt that.[4] Others have questioned this. James Collins and Jerry Porras found that many successful companies started by building a structure and only then determining their strategy.[5] Later writers have also queried whether Chandler's approach is really feasible. Changing the organizational structure is not a cost-free exercise in terms of either money or time. In an era of rapid change when strategic flexibility is essential and it is almost inevitable that strategies will have to change rapidly in order to react to changes in the business environment, can companies really afford to change their organizations every time there is a strategic change? Will they be able to do so quickly enough? And what about the cost to human resources, of almost continuously having to recruit skilled personnel to meet new needs while at the same time making redundant those who are no longer needed?

A more nuanced view was advanced by Raymond Miles and Charles Snow, who showed that strategy, structure and technology are all closely interconnected and that each depends on the other. Specifically, an organization's strategy is constrained, at least to some degree, by the nature of the existing organizational structure and the technology the organization has available to do the job at hand. Of course structures can be changed and new technology required, but sometimes the cost of doing so will be too high, higher than the expected income yielded by the completed strategy if successful (and, too, most businesses understimate the costs of both organizational change and acquiring and integrating new technology). Miles and Snow coined the term 'organizational fitness for purpose' to reflect this need for balance.[6] The right organization is the one that will, practically and effectively, support the optimal strategy and make best use of available technology. However, the optimal strategy should be chosen with the competencies and capabilities of the organization firmly in mind.

Asking questions about organization relating to the spider chart (Figure 6.4 opposite) helps determine initial organizational needs. But then, and continuously as time passes, managers must ask and answer these questions as well:

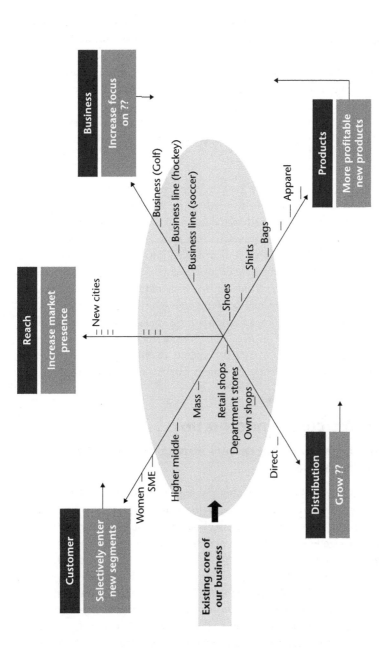

FIGURE 6.4 Proposed strategic direction

1. Does our organizational structure match the current and likely future needs of the organization? If not, what changes should we be looking to make?
2. Do we have enough people with the right skills and competencies in the right areas? Are we deploying our human resources as effectively as we should?
3. Are we compensating people at the right level for the work they do? Are they motivated to do their best for the business and help make sure it meets its goals?

Once more it is important that these question are not asked once only. They need to keep being asked and answered and the answers analysed. This is true even if – especially if – the business is doing well and growing rapidly. Growth brings its own pressures, and as new business units are created and others grow and expand it is vital that they remain linked into the larger organizational framework. One key requirement of any framework is that it should be able to accommodate growth – and indeed, that it should encourage and stimulate growth. Even in times of merely steady growth, there can be a tendency towards complacency and organizational drift. Managers need to monitor the health of the organization on an ongoing basis, using information provided by the framework. If the organization becomes weak, then its ability to deliver on customer promises and execute its strategy can become compromised.

BOX 6.2 CONNECTING THE DOTS . . .

How organizational drivers impact on other drivers and vice versa

Portfolio drivers: As discussed above, there is a fundamental relationship between strategy and structure. If the company has set up in new countries or has set up a new business line or distribution channel, then the organization might have to add new business units and appoint a new management team to run these new units. Similarly if it decides to sell or fix a unit by delayering, then the 'org chart' has to shrink as well.

Marketing drivers: If the organization is going to deliver on the promises made to customers, then it needs to expand and upgrade its organizational and personal capabilities to (a) more skilled production and service people who can make, sell and deliver the right products to the right people; and

(b) an organization that enables staff to execute their duties towards customers in an effective manner. This is vital in all industries but especially so in service industries where staff are in direct contact with customers for much of the time. The back office functions must support the front-of-house, not dictate to it. It might also have to introduce a different training and management development programme or set a new incentive scheme to 'pay' for better customer satisfaction ratings.

Operational drivers: Production, purchasing, supply chain management and above all IT support need to be integrated smoothly into the organization, not treated as separate silos. They must work together in order to achieve a smooth and seamless process of production from purchasing all the way to sales. The value chain approach advocated by Michael Porter shows how all the elements of the business combine together to add value for the customer slim[7]. But this will only happen if the organization facilitates such smooth working together and if staff are well trained and motivated and when there is clarity about roles and responsibility.

Reputational drivers: Organization affects reputation in several ways. First, if an organization is inefficient, this will get noticed. Inefficiency can manifest itself in several ways, from poor service to customers – which affects brand and hence reputation – to sloppy procedures. Second, when there is not the right balance between a sales focused performance culture and the ethical and value performance culture, the company might soon run into reputational risks. This can lead to environmental disasters (such as the *Deepwater Horizon* catastrophe), fraudulent or criminal activity by employees, bribery, corruption, fatal accidents or any of a number of other incidents which could damage the company's reputation. Second, a badly organized company riven by in-fighting and factions – such as the case of steelmaker Corus in the 1990s, where managers in one division threatened legal action against managers in another division over a disagreement about future strategy – will also damage reputation. An organization's reputation depends in part on how unified it is and whether there is a drive to meet ethical values and standards.

Financial drivers: With a well structured reporting and control system, as well as when sound risk and financial management is well embedded into the organization, the company can become more effective. Good control and reporting will also help to prevent reputational damage as referred to above.

Who is really in charge – line or function?

As well as remembering that there is no one best form of organization, we also need to recognize that there is no one most important *part* of any organization. Quite often – too often – we see struggles for control within the organizational matrix. Sometimes functions – especially finance or marketing – become very powerful and their senior managers dominate strategy and policy. Against this, line managers in the business units argue that it is they who generate the profits that grow the company, whereas the functions are merely centres of cost.

So which is more important, line or function? The answer is usually that 'it depends'! Let us take two examples, one of a line manager – the CEO of a business unit – and the other a function manager, the head of HR (the latter having a cost budget, those costs being recharged to other business units or functions).

Here it might look as if the line manager is the most important, the one who calls the shots. But in fact the line manager also needs the support provided by the HR manager. Considering that managers do encourage people to think and act as equal members of the 'one' team with the same end-goals, it is important to frame the relevant issues. Within a matrix setting, it should be recognized that there is always a form of *joint responsibility* and therefore it should be clear who is *primarily* responsible and who is *secondarily* responsible for a certain budget or task. Instead of declaring, as most people tend to do, that the business unit (line) manager is primarily responsible, the better answer is again, that 'it depends' what the question is!

Thus, let us see what question are we trying to ask here. If the question is, who is primarily responsible for *designing* the HR, risk or IT policy for the company, then of course the respective *functional* manager has the primary responsibility, with the line manager having a secondary responsibility. But if the question is, who is primarily responsible for *executing* the policy, the answer is the *line* manager. The functional manager has in this case the secondary responsibility. This means that different people have different responsibilities – but taken together, they have joint responsibility for making sure that things happen. They are both players on the same team, and share the same goals. If all managers involved in setting and executing the strategy understand their joint responsibilities clearly, and if the frameworks list and connect all the dots, then the organization will become much more efficient and effective.

Some companies try to address misalignment between units and departments by installing various committees and 'boards'. They also seek to bring people together across the company in group team-building events. Soon these committees and events become another source of misalignment. Since most committees are not empowered to decide ('they don't have guns and they can't shoot . . .'), delays and misunderstandings are more the rule than the exception. Nokia have installed a series of cross-functional committees and boards to unlock internal silos. A 'brand board' discussed broad issues relating to branding, and a 'capability board' looked at IT investments, while a 'sustainability and environment board' monitored Nokia's green credentials. The result was to slow down rather than speed up decision-making. 'Too many things were coming through headquarters before they were going back out', said one report.[8]

All management layers are involved

The impact of the overarching management framework is that all management layers and all functional columns adopt the same approach, and work with the same corporate vision and mission, strategic objectives and measures in an integrated and simple manner. They will specify and add their views and facts as needed. They are fully involved and engaged when adding their content into the main domains of strategy, execution and organization. People from all parts and layers of the organization will discuss and 'upload' their input to their relevant templates. Both the line manager and the functional manager will contribute equally but focus on their part and role. The matrix organization becomes in this way a much more effective tool. The roles and responsibilities of head office and regional/local offices will be also become more transparent. The principle in the approach of all units and departments should be to 'lead, support and control, in a balanced way'. At ING Asia Pacific there was some dispute over the role of the regional office and its relationship with the twenty business units in the twelve Asian countries where ING operated. Regional management began to articulate this concept of balanced leadership, support and control. The office made it clear that its own role was not only to control the business units, but also to support or to lead the business in new directions. Each staff member received a teacup at their desk with the slogan 'lead, support and control, in a balanced way' printed on it, so that they would be reminded of this principle every day.

Figure 6.5 shows how a management framework can offer a bird's eye view that allows managers to see what is taking place in other parts of the organization, how their own activities fit into the greater scheme of things and how other parts of the organization are working with the six main drivers for excellence.

In Figure 6.5 the six drivers are shown at the top. On the second line you will see the functions involved and which department is looking after which driver. For example the managers of operations, IT, procurement and operational risk management are *functionally* responsible for the operational driver. But apart from being responsible for their own domain, they will also work closely together with other functional and line managers. Executive management has *line* (primary) responsibility for setting the strategic direction and in the end for the final performance. The dark or light orange dots reflect where the functional and line responsibilities come in.

If we think back to the five strategic dimensions discussed in Chapter 3, each dimension has implications for organization. What line of business is the organization in? Mining, steel-making and other forms of heavy industry require concentrations of equipment and people at production sites; hotel and restaurant chains require dispersed locations so as to reach the largest customer base. Line of business in turn helps determine what

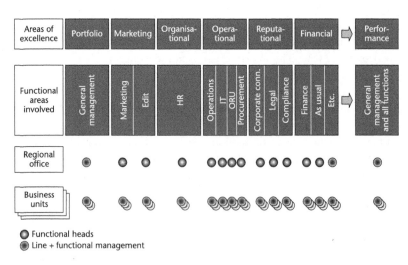

FIGURE 6.5 Managing the framework

products the company makes, or what services it provides, or both; this in turn has implications for the organization, as staff must be deployed in order to support production activities wherever they are needed. Does the company employ physical distribution channels such as retail outlets and warehouses, or virtual channels over the Internet, or some mix of the two? The organization must be structured to support these. Where are the organization's customers and what is its desired reach? Again, the organization must be able to contact and sell to its key customer segments wherever they are.

Answering these questions helps to determine whether the organization is fit for purpose, and if not, where the gaps are and where change is necessary. Again, though, the costs of organizational change and modification have to be balanced against the expected benefit, and it is essential that those costs be accurately estimated. The framework can help provide information about the likely costs of organizational change.

Human resources

Alongside the organizational setting and form, the organizational driver must also take account of the human factor in organizations. Businesses depend on their people to make products, serve customers and execute strategy. Does the business have the right people in the right places at the right time? The key issues to deal with in the framework include skills and competencies, future HR requirements and leadership.

Skills and competencies

We noted above that one of management's primary tasks is to help to build organizational and personal capabilities, rather as coaches help talented players work together to form winning teams. The need for skilled and competent staff throughout the organization will be self-evident. However, one problem which often occurs is deployment. How do we know that we have the *right* people in the *right* place? The problem of putting square pegs into round holes happens far too frequently. The founder and former chairman of Infosys, N. R. Naryana Murthy, reckoned that if an employee was found to be underperforming, the fault might well be with the company. Underperforming employees were offered the chance to transfer to other jobs where their skills might be more relevant, and if this still did not work, they were offered yet another chance. Only after three failures would employees be fired. Murthy estimated that in the great majority of cases, employees were transferred to posts that were more suitable for them, and both they and the company benefitted as result.[9]

Another aspect of the framework, then, is to provide information about what skills and competencies are required for particular posts, thus enabling management to match employees with the optimal posts for them.

Future HR requirements

As well as meeting current needs for skills and competencies, the HR department also has to plan future HR needs. How many employees will be required in future to support growth? The answer depends on the strategic direction of the company, the changing needs of marketing and production, and the scale of growth over a given time period. All of these factors will dictate how many employees will be needed where and when. They will also dictate what skill levels those future employees will need – and depending on the strategic direction, the skill and competency levels of future employees might be very different from those of today. Likewise, if the business is planning to downsize it needs to know which employees are essential and must be retained.

However, HR can only plan effectively if it knows what is going on and what is expected in the rest of the organization. Here is another reason for ensuring that the HR function is fully linked into the framework. Without full knowledge of the strategic direction, without understanding what is happening in marketing, production, finance and elsewhere, HR will be unable to plan accurately.

Leadership

Another important issue is to determine what levels of leadership are required within the organization. This does not necessarily mean top leadership, although issues such as succession planning at the top are doubtless important. Modern theories of leadership such as distributed leadership recognize that leaders are to be found at many different levels and across all parts of the organization, each with a particular responsibility for some part of the business and some part of the strategy.[10] Nonaka and Takeuchi in their book *The Knowledge-Creating Company* regard these lower-level leaders as key drivers of innovation and organizational change.[11] Even if top leadership has responsibility for setting the overall strategic direction, change will not happen if these lower-level leaders are not linked into the organization as a whole.

Management should therefore select, through internal promotion and external recruitment, the right leaders it needs in various parts of the organization, and then ensure that leaders once in place are connected to each other as well as to top leadership, and that there are 'hot lines' that enable them to talk to each other and take concerted action.

This sounds quite easy. The more difficult question is how to find and select the best leaders. Many (good and bad) books and papers have been written about what is good leadership and how to become a great, effective leader or manager. Here, rather than getting into this debate, we prefer to give the reader some concise and easy-to-remember ideas which can be applied when needed. The best leaders are those persons, who are:

1. 'properly wired'; and
2. can operate and function well in the right organizational setting.

Let's drill down a little:

1. 'Properly wired'. In a microchip, if all the elements are well connected through solid wires, the chip will work well, efficiently, reliably and in a trustworthy manner. But in order for this chip to function as part of the whole, it needs to have a proper role and position and be well connected to the rest of the hardware in the computer. Thus the 'properly wired' person should . . .
2. . . . operate and function in the right organizational setting. An excellent soccer player (again if 'properly wired' in terms of physiology and psyche) can only employ his or her skills and competencies to the fullest if they are part of a well-led and capable team.

Compensation

All employees – with the exception of special cases such as volunteers working for charities – require compensation for their efforts. This can take the form of salary, fringe benefits such as health care, insurance, share options and so forth, or some combination of the two. One issue is to determine the optimal level of compensation for employees and managers at different grades and functions. Reward has to be fair, not only to the individual but to others around them who may feel aggrieved if their colleagues are being paid more for the same work.

There is a direct link between compensation and motivation. Employees who feel they are not receiving pay and benefits that are commensurate with the physical and mental effort they expend will suffer a decline in morale and become less effective. They might leave and go to work for competitor organizations, taking valuable knowledge with them. In extreme cases they will become aggrieved and act in ways against the organizations's best interests, such as taking industrial action or pilfering company property. Thus if they are not supported by the right level of compensation and incentives, people will soon cease to be motivated. This could destroy both their own value and that of the company.

A well-planned management development and career path can be another form of incentive for people to 'excel' and keep improving their personal capabilities. Therefore this too should be one of the sub-drivers within the organizational driver, and management development programmes should be designed to be consistent with the overall goals of the company. For example, if one of management's strategic priorities is to boost risk management, then its recruitment and leadership development and training programmes should support this objective.

Conclusions

An effective organization is essential if the business is to meet its strategic goals. The organizational drivers tell managers whether the company has an organization that is fit for purpose, in terms of both organizational structure, reporting, controls and communications, and of the deployment of properly skilled and competent people. Again, this information needs to be made available throughout the organization, not bottled up in the HR department.

In this chapter the organizational driver has been discussed and explained. The key message is that through this driver, leaders have to set as their overriding ambition and goal to constantly improve the personal and organizational capabilities of the *entire* organization, not just the top 10 per cent or an elite group of high achievers, but everyone. Only then can the company create the conditions in which it can excel and outperform the competition.

In order to do so, it is important to define the organizational priorities and sub-priorities, like leadership development, fair compensation, balanced incentive schemes, and a programme to drive a result and ethical performance culture, meeting the requirements of all stakeholders both inside and outside the company. We have also emphasized the importance of clarity, in particular the ability to explain in simple words what the difference is between line and functional responsibilities in a matrix format.

The importance of people is particularly important when we come to examine the next driver, the operational driver. Although technology plays a larger role than ever in operations, with everything from robots making cars and other products in factories to automated voice recognition systems that allow people to shop or pay bills by telephone, all these systems have to be designed and set up by people. There may be fewer people working on shop floors today than a hundred years ago, but those people are far more highly skilled and the individual contribution each makes is far higher. Operations is about people at least as much as, if not more than, technology.

7

THE OPERATIONAL DRIVER

Operations is sometimes described as the heart of the business. We define operations here as the facilities that produce goods and services, complete with ancillary functions such as purchasing and quality control and related functional support operational units. These include functions such as IT, procurement, operational risk management and so on. For the management framework, the operations driver can and should include all the key company operational issues, i.e. it should connect all the operational 'dots'. If for example the company has started an initiative to outsource production to locations in India or China, then this initiative should be listed under the operations driver. Listed too should be all relevant details on how outsourcing will be carried out, when, and who will take responsibility for the process. Depending on the company, what it makes/sells and who its customers are, issues that can be listed under this driver include production, IT, quality control, procurement/purchasing, customer support and operational risk management.

BOX 7.1 OPERATIONAL DRIVERS

- Operations
- Information technology
- Operational risk management
- Procurement

The operational drivers are important because they tell the rest of the company what is possible in terms of design and production. This should help managers to manage the expectations of stakeholders, especially customers. Marketing can then deflect unreasonable or unrealistic requests for services, and concentrate on those core segments who want and need what the business has to offer.

As before, let us first look at what an example of how one might set strategic priorities for operations. Figure 7.1 shows the six drivers, with operations in the lower left hand corner. Each business unit should then set out its operational priorities under the categories given here. Figure 7.2 then shows an example of what a list of priorities might look like, and Figure 7.3 then 'drills down' into the sub-drivers to show priorities can be made more specific and detailed.

The fashion retailer Zara is an example of a firm which makes operational excellence a priority. Zara's strategy is based on its ability to bring the newest trends in fashion to the market in the shortest time possible, faster than most of its competitors. This strategy was built on a vision suggesting that there was a huge market to be captured if the company could respond to the demand for 'I want it now!', and not 'I want it 6–12 months from now', which was how the industry had operated previously. Kids who see their idol on MTV wearing a new t-shirt or jeans want to have the same clothes, and also want to be the first to show their friends

Portfolio	Marketing	Organizational
1. Double digit organic growth 2. Active portfolio management (M&A), including better allocation of capital 3. More and stronger partnerships	4. Introduce profitable new product offerings 5. Increase profitable multi-channel sales 6. Develop strategy for youngsters and women 7. Strengthen customer satisfaction	8. Expand organisational capabilities, including management development 9. Improve performance culture
Operational	**Reputation**	**Financial**
10. Increase efficiency and distributor/customer satisfaction 11. Improve operational risk management 12. Obtain/maintain satisfactory audit rating	13. Increase brand recognition 14. Strengthen compliance 15. Communicate clearly to internal/external stakeholders 16. Ensure integrity, ethical behaviour in all areas	17. Raise $ capital + debt 18. Expand value-based management 19. Strengthen risk mgt 20. Improve MIS & control

FIGURE 7.1 Strategic priorities

Towards performance excellence →

Port → Mkt → Rep → Perf
Port → Org → Fin → Perf
Ops

Illustrative: Please update this slide with strategic priorities for your business unit

Strategic priorities

1. Increase efficiency and distributor/customer satisfaction

2. Improve operational risk management

3. Obtain/maintain satisfactory audit rating and AO scan results

---

Key Ops and IT themes for the region are:
- Operations/IT and related functions to be well aligned with overall ING/IAP strategy and strategic priorities
- Increase efficiency and distributor/customer satisfaction through:
  - Straight-through-processing
  - Agent/customer self-service
  - Implementing optimized customer service model
  - Growing lean six sigma methodology

Operational excellence
●●●○○

FIGURE 7.2 Operational strategic priorities

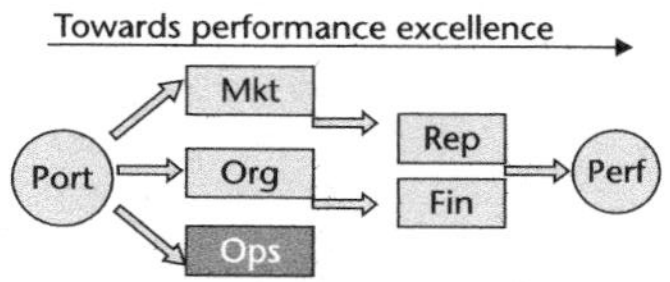

Towards performance excellence →

Driver	Present	Objectives and measures			
	'06E	'07F	'08F	'09F	
Infrastructure • **Lifecycle management** • Nominate any significant upgrades planned to your infrastructure during 2007. (Indicate likely quarter) • **Co-existence** • Indicate any plans for migrating to the new global co-existence environment (GDIL) once it is agreed. • **Compliance to policies affecting infrastructure** • Implementation of email archiving (KVS) • Implementation of Laptop encryption	• Project 1 (Quarter) • Project 2 (Quarter) • Details • Year and quarter • Year and quarter				
Procurement • **Products and tools** • List any planned significant investments in 3rd party tools planned for 2007. Name the product type and likely investment.	• Product – (estimated investment) • Product – (estimated investment) • Product – (estimated investment)				

IT excellence
●●●○○

FIGURE 7.3   Information technology sub–driver

and peers that they 'got it!'. This sense of social and fashion competition amongst young people means that Zara's marketing department is constantly looking for new opportunities and new trends.

However, marketing can only deliver on the strategic promise if it is 'connected' with operations early in the design and production process. Operations in turn is required to move very rapidly through design and production to distribution to retail outlets. In order to achieve this, electronic file and document sharing between all parts of the company, and with suppliers and producers, is crucial. Finance and legal functions are also often involved, and these too must make quick decisions. Some Zara production centres are in its home country, Spain, but others can be in Turkey or South and East Asia. This means that import/export regulations, foreign exchange risk, payments, counter party and operational risk, customer liability, logistics and a whole range of other issues must be considered. The quality control function and customer support centres should also be fully engaged in the process, for these departments will provide many valuable insights into those things which (can) go wrong or which still must be improved. As stated before, one of the key corporate themes has to be 'continuous improvement to outperform the competition'. Many 'dots' have to be connected, in the traditional operations functions but also outside them, before a seamless and efficient process can be put into place.

Let us take another real world example, ING Asia Pacific. Its operations function was initially very dispersed. There was not even a regional operational department to coordinate and share 'best practices'. When the operational managers from the ten countries sat down together for the first time, they started sharing what each of their business units was doing and what they could learn from each other, from both good and bad practice. The next step was to bring the local operational teams together (sometimes in person, most of the time virtually) and divide the work streams into four areas (new business, claims handling, customer support and policies processing). Regional operations manager Bob Epner and his teams then started to look at the key questions. How are we conducting certain activities? What are the underlying efficiency numbers? Why are some units doing certain things one way and not another? How can it become more efficient? Figure 7.4 shows how the operational strategic priorities fit into the overall strategic direction and link with the other drivers.

Epner and his teams then went on to describe how the overall regional operations management function would engage with the ten country businesses to create a single effective process, with clear KPIs established

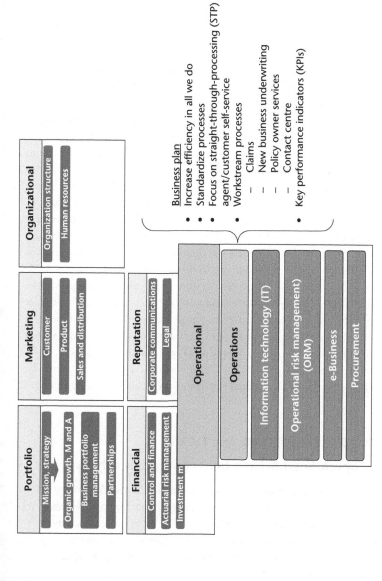

FIGURE 7.4 Planning each aspect of the organization thoroughly

Source: LIMRA magazine, reproduced with kind permission of Bob Epner.

and agreement to drive forward improvements on best practice. It will be seen that there is a balancing of higher quality to meet higher customer satisfactions scores and drive cost down. In a well managed process these are not opposing issues, but will prove to be win–wins.

Unifying diversity

In the ING example, and in most cases where businesses operate across international boundaries, each country is different and each business unit has their own specific set of products, rules and ways of doing things. At the same time, they all belong to the same group of companies, and at the group level managers will be seeking to achieve synergy, cost efficiencies and benefits of scale. In order to achieve these benefits, many companies opt for centralized functions, in operations and in other functions too. This rarely appears to be a real solution. Trying to do everything from the centre will often create even more frictions and tensions. Local staff know their own turf best, and are likely to resent any attempt by head office to tell them how to run things. There is ample evidence that if a company is to be adaptable, flexible, and speedy, there are some things that should be delegated and be empowered to the management at country level, obviously with support from the region and centrally based specialists. The question then becomes one of how to *balance* the obvious benefits of localization with the cost advantages of centralization. In order to have the best of both worlds, there needs to be a way of engaging people at the local level and getting their input into the framework, while regional management steers the process and makes sure everything keeps going forward.

Figure 7.5 shows how at ING, local business units' roles and responsibilities were interwoven with regional functional processes to create a matrix.

BOX 7.2 CONNECTING THE DOTS . . .

How operational drivers impact on other drivers

Portfolio drivers: Take as an example an acquisition of car maker Mini by BMW. It is easy to see that this has had a huge impact on procurement, R&D and sharing technologies, as well as issues such as plant location. Just as with marketing, businesses have to be careful to plan realistically. Portfolio strategy must be conducted within the limits of what the company can deliver.

Marketing drivers: As noted in the main text, marketing must not promise what the rest of the firm cannot achieve. Marketers need to know what production capacity the company has, what distribution and IT capacity it has, and whether the products and services it provides will be reliable and ethically sourced.

Organizational drivers: The organizational structure must support efficient and effective operations, and the HR function must provide operations with skilled and trained staff as and when they are needed. Neither is possible without knowing what the company's operational needs are. The framework must seek to break down the silos separating operations from other functions so that needs can be accurately assessed and met.

Reputational drivers: Lack of effective operations functions will surely have an impact on the company's reputation. Unethical sourcing of products will rebound on the company if the media learn about it. Inefficient and ineffective operations could also produce other events such as industrial accidents, environmental damage and so on, which would be not only a PR disaster but could also put the company in breach of the law. BP's disastrous fire and oil spill in the Gulf of Mexico is an example of an event which harmed the company's reputation on several levels simultaneously.

Financial drivers: Finally, lack of efficiency and effectiveness will impact on financial drivers in terms of increasing costs and decreasing profits and revenues. As noted, an operation can be technically efficient and still generate high profits and revenues. The finance function will want to see an appropriate balance struck.

Elements of the driver

Let us now look at some of the most important individual functions, the sub-drivers within the operational driver.

Information technology

Just as every department has its own purchasing requirements, so every department and business unit also has its own IT requirements. One important requirement here is compatibility. We discussed earlier how different business units develop their own ways of reporting and even their

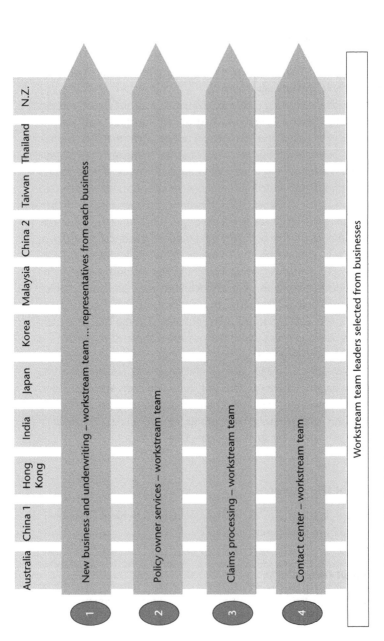

FIGURE 7.5 People: shared leadership is natural

Source: LIMRA magazine, reproduced with kind permission of Bob Epner.

own languages. One frequent cause of this is that business units are using separate and incompatible IT systems. In highly decentralized organizations, business units are often encouraged to do their own IT procuring. The result is that each business unit has an IT system that may work beautifully for itself, but cannot network with the rest of the business. It is essential that all IT systems are compatible and share a common platform. This means that if business units do their own IT sourcing, they should do so to agreed common technical specifications and standards.

The first step is for the business units to exchange information about their current IT capabilities and needs, to enable the company to get a clearer picture of what its IT strategy should be. It does not matter whether IT systems are run in-house or outsourced to an IT service company; this step is equally important in either case. Some IT functions, such as email systems or intranets, will span the entire group, and hence it will be comparatively easy to set up a common group-wide standard. Other IT functions might be decentralized, either regionally or locally or by business unit. This is acceptable, so long as information is readily available and easily shared to support decision-making. Figure 7.6 shows the components of this important driver in more detail.

Operations

'Operations' will of course depend on the nature of the business and its products and customers. Operations can range from mining operations or subsea oil drilling to automobile assembly plants to air traffic control centres to restaurant kitchens to the derivatives trading floors to the offices of insurance companies; indeed, there are thousands of possible permutations. For a manufacturing company such as Ford or Caterpillar, 'operations' refers to the manufacturing process or assembly process in the factory, and also including the network (semi-) independent suppliers. In banking, 'operations' refers to the processing departments that handle mortgages, loans and payments.

The data sets related to the manufacturing and administrative processes can be huge. It is best to begin by *listing* the first high level 'drivers' or initiatives that are relevant in the operational area and especially to connect the dots with the other drivers. Specific and detailed work processes can be left to the production departments themselves through various sub-files. Figure 7.7 gives an example of various elements which could be part of an operations template.

The framework here needs to concentrate on a few key elements: *purpose, effectiveness, efficiency* and *quality*. First, is the operations system oriented towards

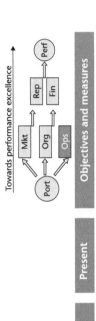

Towards performance excellence

Driver	Present	Objectives and measures			
	'11E	'12F	'13F	'14F	

Driver

Applications and architecture
- **Implementation of IA3**
- What projects and activities will further the roll out of IA3 in your business unit in 2007
- Describe your plans for the IA3 Infohub and operational data store in 2007
- **Reuse of applications**
- *Self side*: applications you have installed or will develop that you believe will be reusable by other business units
- *Buy side*: applications you plan to obtain by reusing existing applications from other business units
- **Standardization of applications**
- Indicate when you plan to implement the following standardized applications:
- PeopleSoft
- Information hub/operational data store
- BPM (TIBCO or FileNet)

Present / Objectives and measures
- Provide a brief description of your program of work in this area
- Highlight any projects that will either implement or extend the infohub and ODS

- Provide a brief description of the application subject area
- Provide a brief description of the application subject area

- Implemented / year and quarter / NA (why)
- Implemented / year and quarter / NA (why)
- Implemented / year and quarter / NA (why)
- Implemented / year and quarter / NA (why)
- Implemented / year and quarter / NA (why)

IT excellence

FIGURE 7.6 Information technology sub–drivers

Towards performance excellence →

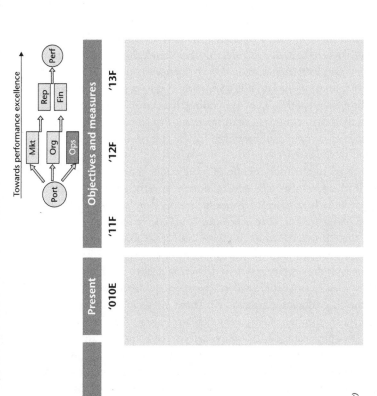

Driver	Present	Objectives and measures			
	'010E	'11F	'12F	'13F	

Production optimization initiatives
- Innovation, R&D
- Quality improvement
- ISO standards
- **Efficiency improvements**
  - material cost/unit
  - labour hours/unit

POS/CC
- Call center interface
- Advanced telephony
- Workflow/BPM

SIX SIGMA
- Lean six sigma workshops
- Orange belts
- Black belts
- Staff for "Train-the-trainers"

Note: Black belt training @ approx. €6,000 and Ops network/
Work stream conference @ approx. €3,000 (3–4 conferences/year)

Operations excellence

FIGURE 7.7 Operational sub–drivers

the strategic goals of the business? Does it support the strategy that is being executed? To take just one example from above: reach; managers need to know where the company's operating systems are located, what kind of geographical reach they have and whether they are ideally suited to supporting the business and its strategic goals. Many financial institutions moved their call centres to India in the late 1990s and early 2000s, but a few are now questioning the wisdom of this. They are finding that customers prefer call centres located in their own countries, with the result that some companies are now establishing 'in-country' call centres to handle at least some functions.

Related to this is effectiveness. Is the operations system doing what it is supposed to do in terms of volume of production, timeliness of production and so on? Managers also need information on the efficiency of the operating system, particularly concerning issues such as spoilage and waste. While we made the point earlier that efficiency and effectiveness do not always coincide, there is still a need to eliminate unnecessary inefficiencies.

Finally, there is the issue of quality and meeting sustainability norms and requirements. Is the operating system delivering quality goods and services to customers – that is, as we discussed in Chapter 5, do the company's goods and services match customer expectations? There are several ways of gathering quality. One is through post-production inspection. This is easier in the production of physical products, when defects can be noted and weeded out before products reach the customer. In services, the tendency instead is to measure complaints, which means that defective or unsatisfactory service has already reached the customer. Today the preferred method is to 'build quality in', looking for targets such as 'six sigma' or 'zero defects'.[1] In order to build quality in, managers are required to design a system which eliminates the possibility of defects occurring in the production system. However, in order to do this managers need accurate information about quality requirements, including technical specifications. They also need to know what production technology the company is using and what are its capabilities.

Procurement

Procurement, or purchasing, is another important area. Several issues need to be covered under this heading. First, what are the company's purchasing requirements? Second, are those requirements being met efficiently and in a timely manner? Third, what future purchasing requirements will need to be met? Figure 7.8 shows how a purchasing department might set out its priorities.

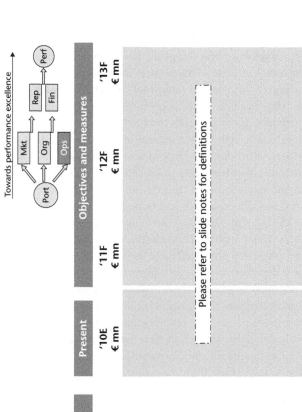

Towards performance excellence →

Driver	Present	Objectives and measures			
	'10E € mn	'11F € mn	'12F € mn	'13F € mn

Total spend
- "% of total spend done through global/regional contracts
- Total controllable spend
  - % controllable spend where procurement is involved
- Total contract spend
  - % of contracts co-signed by procurement and budget owner

Strategic sourcing
- Added value in relation to spend
  - Savings
- % of spend sourced following P&P

Please refer to slide notes for definitions

Note: If the required systems to produce requested data are not available, please state "data not available" and mention when will the system be available to report these KPI's

Procurement excellence

FIGURE 7.8 Procurement

Procurement is often overlooked in strategic thinking, but of course it is vital. Without a steady flow of materials and components, the production system will not work efficiently – or at all. In these days of lean production and Just-in-Time management, most companies keep very limited stocks of components and material in hand. This exposes them to operational risk (see below). Ensuring the continuous inflow of materials is essential to make and deliver the products that meet customer needs. However, purchasing is about much more than raw materials for the factory floor. Back office functions also need their own supplies of everything: stationery, laser printer cartridges, office furniture and much else. Sales people need brochures and literature, either hard copy or soft copy, to show to customers. Every department and every business unit has its own purchasing needs which must be met if that department or unit is to operate effectively. Issues such as low cost v. high quality, discounts on volumes, quality of suppliers, Just-in-Time delivery, group standards, guarantees, co-development and so on are all important issues that may need to be considered.

Therefore, every department and every business unit should have its purchasing needs accurately recorded. Over time, actual purchasing should be monitored against stated purchasing needs, in terms of both quantity of purchasing and timeliness of ordering. Purchasing in insufficient quantities or too late to meet needs at a given time risks creating delays and harming efficiency. On the other hand, purchasing too much too soon can lead to unnecessary wastage. Data from the framework can be used to get the balance right.

And, of course, this balance is always shifting. As the company grows – or contracts – and as it moves to serve new customers in new markets, its purchasing needs will change constantly. It is therefore vital that purchasing data and information are updated on an ongoing basis.

Operational risk and corporate security

We have already made the point that delays, inefficiencies and wastage can cause delays or even bring the operating system to a halt. Management needs to develop contingencies for a variety of events.

Simple mechanical breakdowns are a common cause of operational delays. How can these be best guarded against or prevented? In some countries where the electricity supply is unreliable, power failures are another contingency that must be planned for. Most companies operating in India have backup generators, but one graphics design company divides its work between two centres on opposite sides of the country, so that in the event of a major power failure at least one system can keep operating. This results in duplication, redundant systems and a certain amount of technical inefficiency; but on several occasions in the past, this system has proven a life-saver.

Industrial unrest can be another major source of operational risk, particularly when companies are operating on a Just-in-Time supply basis. In 2003 a strike at a main components supplier to General Motors in Michigan threatened to bring GM's entire American production system to a halt in less than a week if the supply of components dried up. Fortunately the strike was settled quickly and production was able to continue without pause, but the risk was very real.

There is also a need to plan for major disasters. Terrorist attacks on financial districts mean that companies may have to relocate into temporary premises while their own offices are repaired, as happened in New York after the 9/11 attacks. Provision for such temporary office space has to be made in advance. Pandemic illnesses represent another major threat, as widespread illness and absenteeism can seriously harm operations. The World Health Organization has repeatedly warned of the likelihood of a major epidemic of H5N1, better known as bird flu, should this disease become capable of transmission between humans. Some organizations have disaster plans in place to cover a possible absenteeism rate of 50 per cent. Disasters can also affect other companies up and down the supply chain. The Japanse tsunami of 2011 not only killed tens of thousand of people, it destroyed factories producing vital parts for plants elsewhere in Japan, with the result that these businesses had to slow down or even temporarily close.

These may sound like 'black swan' events that no one could predict. Yet, they all happened. The companies that survive these events are those that have disaster plans in place, and where everyone knows their own responsibility in the event of a major incident. Andrew Grove, chairman of Intel, has argued that a degree of 'paranoia' is essential for managers.[2] They should assume that what can go wrong, will go wrong, and be prepared to act accordingly.

Most large multinational companies now have corporate security departments to protect the company, its staff and sometimes its customers against fraud, natural incidents or disasters, assaults and robbery, theft, corporate espionage or terrorism. Figure 7.9 gives an example of how operational risk and corporate security can be integrated into the framework.

Towards performance excellence →

Mkt → Rep → Perf
Port → Org, Ops → Fin

Regional objectives. Please update status of your business unit

Driver	Present '06E	Objectives and measures '07F	'08F	'09F
Corporate security – general				
Training – Develop overall project management abilities and specific security knowledge	July group conference	Industrial certification, external courses, AP training conference, group strategic conference		
Monitoring and reporting – Roll out new group reporting requirements, bi-annual Scorecard, meeting minimum scores for Amber KRI as set by group. Dashboard	MT report – BC/DR Dec; scorecard 21%	Meet 65% scorecard hurdle rate, 6 KRI indicators and dashboard by 1 Jan 07		
Incident reporting – raising awareness senior management and group		Single country indicator		
Personal security				
Safe and secure – events, projects, hotels, travel, country risks, executive protection, expatriate evacuations	Ad-hoc reviews, all events, all projects	Annual review of hotels and venues, big events and projects, country risks		
Incidents handling – use of security firms and emergency procedures	Ad-hoc	Rollout emergency procedures and contact number, annual review of security firms		
Physical security				
Secure and safe – premises, transportation, assets and valuables	Re-assess risks	Annual risks assessment, area & assets classification, management of premises, fire protection measures, intruder detection, access control. Annual fire drills.		
Monitor and checking – monthly clean desks, intrusion, fire drills				
Crisis Management				
Organisational – setup CMO & SMT	Setup SMT Distribute emergency procedures	Increase planning, perform BIA, review and test plans per 2 yr test cycle, annual fire drill, semi-annual CCP		
Planning – complete impact and planning	Perform fire drills			
Testing – all plans				
Anti-fraud				
Policy – roll out when issued by group	Anti-phising risk assess Reaffirm policy and procedures	Complete implementation by 31 March 07 PES for all staff		
Anti-phishing – risks assessment, implementation	Remediate SOX	Remediate SOX according to group policy		
PES – all staff / Please refer to slide notes		setup SIU		
SOX q's 70 & 46				
Incident & response				

Corporate security excellence

FIGURE 7.9 Corporate security

BOX 7.3 A PARADIGM SHIFT IN COST AND SELLING PRICE

In general companies have their standard way of strategic thinking about cost of operations and then setting the sales price. Up to recently the frame of mind or the economic formula was:

$$Cost + margin = > price$$

Richard Branson of Virgin turned the formula upside down by setting the price as low as possible to attract a whole new customer segment of low budget travellers and then re-engineer all steps in the service and production process in such a way that cost dropped so much that acceptable margins would still result.

In most markets the long tail is in the mass markets. People are 'under sold' to. Thanks to the Internet millions more choices have become available. Think of books and music and indeed at very low prices. Many (fast growing) companies nowadays apply the formula in the opposite direction, being:

$$price = > cost + margin$$

In this way it can be seen how important it is to determine what the interdependencies and the strategic merits can be if one is capable of thinking outside of the box and approaching the issue from a totally different angle.

All managers, not just operations managers, need to be able to ask and have answered the following questions:

1. How can operations support the strategic direction? Are they generating the high quality, innovative products that customers want?
2. What are our purchasing needs, and are we meeting them effectively?
3. Does our IT capability match the needs of the organization?
4. What operational risks do we face and what measures are in hand to deal with them?

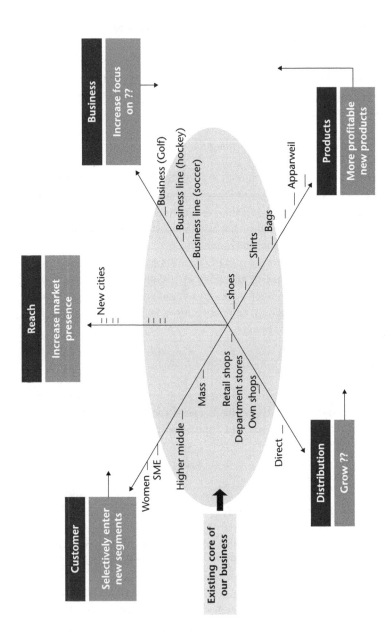

FIGURE 7.10 The operations dimension and strategy

Business
Increase focus on ??

Business (Golf)
Business line (hockey)
Business line (soccer)

Products
More profitable new products

Apparweil
Bags
Shirts
shoes

Reach
Increase market presence

New cities

Customer
Selectively enter new segments

Women
SME
Higher middle
Mass

Retail shops
Department stores
Own shops

Existing core of our business

Direct

Distribution
Grow ??

Each of these questions is important for its own reason. The first, as noted above, impacts directly on the ability of the company to meet its strategic goals. But the ability of the company to produce good quality, innovative products depends in turn on its ability to source raw materials and components in an effective manner. Again, this does not necessarily mean the cheapest components and materials. Quality products must be made from quality parts. Further, in these days of increasing social and environmental awareness on the part of consumers and the public in general, companies' purchasing activities are coming under greater scrutiny. Coffee shop chains are being asked to source coffee beans from Fair Trade producers, and restaurants that offer organically grown food are often able to command a price premium. Conversely, companies that source clothing from 'sweat-shops' in Asia will suffer reputational damage if this comes to light.

IT platforms and systems must be capable of supporting the activities of the business. These systems do not generate revenue in and of themselves; they are a cost, and need to be managed accordingly. During the late 1990s, many companies spent millions on IT systems without really knowing what they were buying. Later studies concluded that few if any of these companies would recoup the full cost of their investment.

Finally, companies must know what operational risks they face and what the consequences could be if potential threats do materialize. Again, these questions need to be asked continually, not just as one-off events. Knowing how the company's operations have changed is vital to other managers when setting out their plans.

BOX 7.4 EFFICIENCY AND EFFECTIVENESS

An optimal operation is one that helps the company deliver on its strategy efficiently and effectively. It is important that both of these terms are borne in mind. *Efficiency* means at the least possible cost, while *effectiveness* means in a manner that creates the greatest value.

The two terms are not always synonymous, and sometimes a technically inefficient operation is actually more effective. For example, it might be thought that running a train or bus service with a 100 per cent occupancy rate for seats is the most efficient way of doing so. This might be true in terms of revenue generation in the short term, but trains and buses that are always 100 per cent full are likely to be overcrowded and uncomfortable. Also, there are likely to be other customers who wanted to use the train or bus but could not, and they will become disgruntled and spread bad reports about the operating company. Hotels know this too, and some hotel chains take care not to book all of their rooms in advance, leaving some free for customers who arrive at the last minute.

Conclusions

Operations are what keeps the company going, and are an integral part in the total process of achieving performance excellence. Through operations, products and services are made and delivered and a variety of ancillary and support functions are provided. There is no doubting the fact that without an efficient and effective operations function, nothing or not enough will happen as it should.

Yet, as we have seen above, much can go wrong in operations, and when it does the consequences can be severe. Mistakes, errors, wastage and disasters all affect the company's reputation. In extreme cases they can result in legal and regulatory violations which can cost the company dearly, both in financial terms and in terms of image. We shall turn to reputational drivers in the next chapter.

8

THE REPUTATION DRIVER

A company might have a superbly crafted strategy and a fine organization, and it might excel at marketing or operations. But if it does not perform well in areas like communications or if it is confronted with major legal disputes or involved in *unethical* behaviours like price-fixing, fraud and bribery, it risks facing negative effects from customers and other stakeholders. We call this reputation management, which forms our fifth driver. But reputation management goes further. Through effective internal and external communication, including building a reputable brand, good public relations, etc., the company can create substantial shareholder value over time.

BOX 8.1 REPUTATION DRIVERS

- Corporate communications
- Legal affairs
- Compliance
- Integrity and ethics

Companies need to manage their communications and reputation if they are to avoid these negative effects. Yet there is also a more positive side if the reputation driver is managed well. Through effective internal and external communication, including building brands and good public relations, the company can create substantial brand equity and shareholder value over time.

Indeed, managing reputation is high on the agenda of most CEOs. According to a survey of 200 companies conducted by the PR firm Hill & Knowlton and the search firm Korn & Ferry, nearly two-thirds of CEOs of these companies say it is one of their key objectives to manage the company's reputation.

Figure 8.1 shows the set of sub-drivers that rests inside the reputational driver, at the bottom centre of the overall chart, and also shows the relationship of the reputational driver to the other five. Figure 8.2 shows the strategic priorities of the reputation driver in more detail.

In the words of Benjamin Franklin, 'it takes many good deeds to build a good reputation, and only one bad one to lose it'. Customers, employees, governments, investors and the public at large are unforgiving of mistakes by businesses – perhaps more so now than ever before. Companies can literally live and die by their reputations. Years spent building a great reputation can be wiped out in a moment.

Consider the case of Gerald Ratner, who built up a small family business to become the world's largest jewellery retail chain. His business was highly

Portfolio	Marketing	Organizational
1. Double digit organic growth 2. Active portfolio management (M&A), including better allocation of capital 3. More and stronger partnerships	4. Introduce profitable new product offerings 5. Increase profitable multi-channel sales 6. Develop strategy for youngsters and women 7. Strengthen customer satisfaction	8. Expand organisational capabilities, including management development 9. Improve performance culture
Operational	**Reputation**	**Financial**
10. Increase efficiency and distributor/customer satisfaction 11. Improve operational risk management 12. Obtain/maintain satisfactory audit rating	13. Increase brand recognition 14. Strengthen compliance 15. Communicate clearly to internal/external stakeholders 16. Ensure integrity, ethical behaviour in all areas	17. Raise $ capital + debt 18. Expand value-based management 19. Strengthen risk mgt 20. Improve MIS and control

FIGURE 8.1 Strategic priorities

Strategic priorities
1. Increase brand recognition
2. Strengthen compliance
3. Communicate clearly with internal/external stakeholders
4. Ensure integrity and ethical behaviour in all areas

FIGURE 8.2   Reputational strategic priorities

valued by investors and he himself was lauded by politicians and business leaders alike for his success. Then came a single moment of madness. In a speech widely reported by the British media, Ratner began making jokes about his company's products and referred to one of them as 'crap'. This was treated as evidence of contempt for customers. There was a media frenzy, investors began to back away and the share price slid to 10 per cent of its original value. Eventually Ratner was forced out of the company by his own board, and the original Ratner company went into liquidation. A multinational company was killed by a fifteen-minute speech.

Reputation threats take many forms. There is the hubris that leads people like Ratner to say foolish things that damage their own business. There is the possibility that managers and staff may behave inappropriately or incorrectly towards customers – as in the case of the mis-selling of pensions that cost many British financial service companies very dearly in the 1990s – or towards each other. Mechanical failure in the workplace can cost lives or lead to environmental pollution. Products, once sold to customers, may fail or break down and cause injury or death. People may bend the rules or even break them in pursuit of goals of their own, as happened in the cases of Jérôme Kerviel or Nick Leeson. Even when there is no law-breaking, people may behave in ways that contravene the company's own code of conduct, with negative consequences for its reputation.

Protection of reputation is vital because, in order for people to do business with a company, they have to trust it. Customers need to believe that the products they buy will satisfy their needs, and certainly need to believe that they will not be actively harmful. Employees need to know that the company will treat them fairly and provide them with a safe working environment. Investors need to know that the company is sound and well-financed and contains no lurking financial black holes. Governments and society at large need to know that the company is working for the interests of society as a whole, not just seeking profit for its own ends and ignoring the cost to others. If things go wrong with any one of these stakeholders, the rest will soon get to hear about it. Blogs, Twitter, Facebook and other communications channels will spread the word like wildfire.

As we saw in Chapter 5, reputation and brand are closely linked and part of a company's brand equity, especially with external communication activities, and reside in the reputation it has with various stakeholder groups. Reputation drivers must therefore make up an important part of any management framework.

Building and maintaining reputation

Figure 8.3 reminds us of the five strategic dimensions. It should be clear that reputation is involved in each one of these dimensions: in meeting customer needs, in delivering quality products in timely fashion and so on. Companies build and maintain their reputation all the time, through the hundreds of initiatives they take and things that they do – or sometimes, the things that they *don't* do. General Electric has a policy of hiring only the best staff and training them thoroughly. It thus gains the reputation of being a company where ambitious people want to work. Its image as a successful, high-performing organization is reflected in the recruitment market value of former GE employees. The same is true of former employees of some of the large management consultancies such as BCG or McKinsey. Similarly, if a company or institution has a clear and well-enforced anti-bribery policy and is known to be an organization of high integrity, this will become known and will add to the company's reputation.

If the company wants to build and maintain a solid reputation, managers need constantly to look at four issues and need to have answers to some key questions such as:

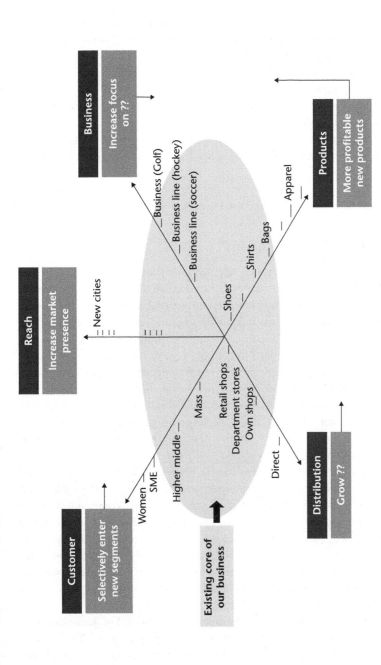

FIGURE 8.3 Reputation and strategic position

1. Corporate communications: are we sending a clear and consistent message to our stakeholders? In particular, are we communicating our *brand* values clearly to stakeholders?
2. Legal issues: are we in strict compliance with the law and regulations in each jurisdiction where we operate?
3. Compliance: do all staff in all business units comply with our own codes of conduct and other internal regulations?
4. Integrity and ethical behaviour: do all leaders, managers and staff at all levels fully understand what is needed to avoid the risks of unethical behaviour?

Let us now consider each of these four issues in turn.

Corporate communications

Corporate communications is usually associated with PR, but in fact encompasses much more than that. The domain of corporate communications includes all channels of internal and external communication between a company and with its stakeholders – and arguably could include advertising, which is usually seen as the province of the marketing department. Again, we need to consider how to break down silos and list and order all things that a company wants to get done to achieve performance excellence. It is indeed very important that advertising and other corporate communications do not send out conflicting messages. It may be appropriate for the marketing department to administer advertising campaigns, but other parts of the company need to see them and be aware of them.

Corporate communications have a twofold task. First, they transmit the vision, mission, strategic position and direction, priorities and *values* of the company, as described in Chapter 3. They communicate these aspects to customers, employees and other stakeholders in a way such that all know what the company stands for. Second, they communicate the company's *purpose*. They explain, both internally as externally, what the company is trying to do and why, and what the benefits will be. For example, communication with employees through newsletters, intranets and the like should aim to make employees aware of what is happening around the company and what is expected of them personally in order to help the business achieve its strategic goals. The same is true of external communications with investors, shareholders, regulators, suppliers, partners, media and of course current and potential customers. In each case it is important that the company tell its own story.[1] (If it does not, then there is a risk that others such as competitors or rivals may start telling stories instead.)

In terms of the management framework there are two requirements. One is to ensure that everyone is aware of what corporate communications functions such as PR, internal relations and so on are doing and what messages are being sent to stakeholders. The other is to ensure that the right messages *are* being sent. In large and complex organizations it is easy for corporate communications functions to multiply, and then there is always the risk that conflicting messages will go out. It is very important that the business communicates a single clear and consistent set of messages about itself.

Getting to the specifics

Let us look at the specific actions and initiatives that can be listed for the company to check whether it needs them to drive and execute the reputation driver. Figure 8.4 gives examples of the kinds of initiatives necessary for an effective internal and external communication process. Note that the focus here is on keeping staff and external stakeholders properly informed, and not only on the channels of communication themselves. There are many, many different channels and media that can be used – conferences, meetings with analysts and investors, sponsoring, marketing materials, intranets, corporate websites, Facebook, Twitter and other social networking sites, staff magazines, internal 'city council' or 'town hall' meetings – and the choice of which methods to use will depend on the stakeholder group, the message to be communicated, and indeed the company's own culture and ethos.

The list of activities in Figure 8.4 will also help the company to establish the cost of these various measures, and to measure their effectiveness over time. If cost-cutting becomes necessary, then it is an easy matter to go through the list of actions and decide which activities can be cut or reduced.

Branding

There might be quite some debate about whether strong brands like BMW or McDonald's are the result of years of great company performance and

Towards performance excellence →

Communications	Present	Objectives and measures		
	'06F	'07F	'08F	'09F
Internal communications • Internal publication • Production cost (€ '000s)	• Name/audience • Cost of total production (incl. headcount)	• Changes to be implemented? XXX	XXX	XXX
Media relations • Media relations support • Communications planning • Crisis management plan	• Agency used • Not previously reported	XXX • Initiatives in place? • Initiatives in place?	XXX	XXX
Marketing material • Corporate spend • Product spend • Other	• (€ '000s) • (€ '000s) • (€ '000s)	XXX XXX XXX	XXX XXX XXX	XXX XXX XXX
Corporate responsibility • Chances for children target • Environment • Ad-hoc initiatives	• Not previously reported	XXX • Initiatives in place? • Initiatives in place?	XXX	XXX
Corporate events • Customer focused • Sales force focused	• Not previously reported	XXX XXX	XXX XXX	XXX XXX

Communication excellence

FIGURE 8.4 Corporate communications

millions of ongoing satisfied customers, or merely of smart brand campaigning. Of course the answer might be both. In the two cases just mentioned it might be that customers are happy with the great performance of BMW cars and the great value for money of McDonald's and this builds brand value. But if we look at examples of luxury brands such as Louis Vuitton, Hermès or Gucci, the main contributor might well be the vast amounts spent on smart positioning and branding in the opening of glamorous shops at prime locations in cities such as New York and Tokyo. Nike and Apple also have some of the same characteristics of well-known fashion brands.

In Figure 8.5 some of the activities of building a brand are listed. Programmes for staff to improve customer satisfaction (also listed under the marketing driver) and measuring customer responsiveness are initiatives which management can take as part of a branding strategy. Advertising and sponsorship are important too. Which will better support the company's brand, sponsoring the New York Marathon or investing in Formula 1 racing? These are questions which should be discussed not only by the marketing and communication departments but also by top management.

There should be an interactive process between corporate communication and branding, since they can strengthen each other. Moreover all departments should be fully engaged and support the reputational programmes. For example if clients are not happy, it will harm the brand and vice versa. All people involved should 'live the brand' especially when customers are involved. This even applies to the smallest details. For example, when a customer has to wait a couple of minutes too long before they get the right (capable and empowered) person on line or if they do not get timely and proper answers to emails sent, the reputation of the company will soon start to deteriorate.

As Franklin said, it takes a long time to build a reputation. It is very easy to proclaim that one's company is honest and virtuous and is working for the benefit of all its stakeholders. But stakeholders will not necessarily believe this. They want proof; they want actions rather than words. They will judge a company in part by what it says through corporate communications, but in much larger part by its actions. Trust can take a long time to build.

As we saw in Chapters 5 and 7, it is vital that a company develops a reputation for making products that meet customer needs and for delivering them in a timely fashion to the right place, as Zara has done so

Towards performance excellence

Branding	Present	Objectives and measures		
	'06F	'07F	'08F	'09F
Customer centricity				
• Customer satisfaction	• Current	XX%	XX%	XX%
• Brand attributes	• Current	XX%	XX%	XX%
• Treats me fairly	• Current	XX%	XX%	XX%
• Easy to deal with	• Current	XX%	XX%	XX%
• Delivers on promises				
• CCAP actions	• Key project 1	• Outcome of project in 2007 and means of measurement		
(people, products, processes, communication)	• Key project 2	• Outcome of project in 2007 and means of measurement		
	• Key project 3	• Outcome of project in 2007 and means of measurement		
Brand strategy				
• Brand awareness	• Calculated from latest review	XX%	XX%	XX%
• Aided	• Calculated from latest review	XX%	XX%	XX%
• Unaided				
• Country brand status	• In line with group strategy?	• List exceptions to use of ING <Lion> (only) brand		
• Introduce brand signature		• Timeline for brand signature implementation		
Advertising spend				
• Products ad (€ '000s)	• Agreed to increase spend by at least 10% per annum	XXX	XXX	XXX
• Corporate ad (€ '000s)		XXX	XXX	XXX
• Total as % of new business	• % in	X%	X%	X%
Sponsorship (€ '000s)	• Detail local sponsorship projects	XXX	XXX	XXX

Communication excellence

FIGURE 8.5 Branding activities

successfully. These two factors will play an important role in generating satisfaction and trust among customers. It helps too if the company has a reputation associated with a certain line of business: Apple with consumer electronics, BMW with cars, Hilti with power tools, and so on. These reputations create associations in the minds of customers and other stakeholders. In the end what here applies is that 'reputation is the power of the message'.

Just as the company itself must have reach, so must its reputation. A reputation built up painstakingly over years in one market will be of no value when the company expands into new markets, unless it can also also extend the reach of its reputation into that market. Starbucks has been able to expand into many markets around the world because its strong reputation had for the most part preceded it into those markets. Customers were aware of the Starbucks brand and the bundle of benefits it offered. Other companies in other markets have struggled to achieve market entry because they had no reputation. Customers knew nothing about these companies – or else what they did know was wrong – and accordingly saw no reason to switch from the brands they were already buying.

Let us take an example – the Indian-based conglomerate the Tata group. Tata is the oldest and largest private sector business group in India. It also has India's most valuable corporate brand – and one of the most valuable in the world – plus a large suite of product and service brands. The Tata brand relies heavily on its reputation for trust. From its foundation in 1868, the Tata group has stuck to its core values of providing goods that will benefit consumers, creating wealth and doing good in the communities where it operates. Decades of sticking to this recipe have made Tata a highly respected and trusted name in India, and that in turn has been a key factor in the company's growth and prosperity. This extends right across all stakeholder groups: customers know that they can trust Tata products, employees know that Tata companies and managers will treat them fairly, and so on. So strong is this reputation that when mistakes do occur – as they inevitably do – people are willing to be forgiving because they know that Tata group will make good any problems that occur.

This was made very clear in 2002 when the group's finance operation, Tata Finance, was found to have a 'black hole' of unknown size. The company collapsed, and its managing director and several other executives were arrested on suspicion of fraud. This was potentially a dangerous moment; a company that everyone knew and trusted now had an Enron-style problem. Group chairman Ratan Tata knew he had to take immediate action. 'Once you lose your reputation for trust', he said, 'nothing else matters.' In an unprecedented move he stated publicly that all the losses suffered by clients of Tata Finance would be made good by money coming from elsewhere in the group. The losses eventually totalled more than $300 million, but Tata kept its word and every penny was repaid.[2]

This happened in India. Now that the Tata group is extending its reach and expanding into the larger world, however, it is finding it very difficult to leverage that reputation in new markets. One of the group's companies, watch-maker Titan, is India's leading watch-maker and has achieved some extraordinary breakthroughs in engineering including the world's thinnest watch, the edge, little thicker than a sheet of paper. But when Titan attempted to expand into the UK and America, it met with a cool reception. Customers there had never heard of Titan and associated Indian engineering with second-rate, inferior work. Titan was forced to sell its stores in both countries and retreat to India. A great and shining reputation in one country meant nothing in another. Conscious of this, Tata kept its own brand out of the picture when acquiring famous brands like Jaguar and Land Rover, and manages these as 'stand alone' brands.

Legal affairs

In general one can state that each and every action might have legal consequences. Whether it actually will depends on the country and the culture in which one operates. The USA has a highly legalistic culture, China less so. Big international companies may spend tens or even hundreds of millions of dollars a year on legal fees. Yet this is money well spent; spending money on legal work in advance can help to avoid far larger costs in terms of claims or losses down the road. Therefore it is important that the legal sub-drivers are complete, coherent and comprehensive, aligned with all aspects and departments/business units in the company. For example, if a new partnership is being considered or a new product brought to market, the legal issues should be properly discussed and documented before the process starts.

The first step is to ensure that people understand the legal context within which they are operating. They also need to know the legal structure of the company or group. Are brands, trademarks and patents properly protected? What contractual arrangements does the company have with employees, suppliers, distributors, banks? It should be clear that answering these questions involves reaching out to and connecting with many other 'dots', right across the company (see Figure 8.6).

Compliance

One of the purposes of the reputation driver is to assist and ensure that certain laws will apply to what the company does (or even doesn't do) and what it is required to do to comply. Again, this must be a constant process as in most jurisdictions laws are constantly changing and new laws being promulgated. Moreover it should be done at all levels of the company and by all persons, since their actions (or lack thereof) could unnecessarily expose the company to all kinds of risk. All companies in all jurisdictions are required to comply with national and local law. Often there will be several layers of laws and regulations: country law, city laws or by-laws, regulations promulgated by industry bodies which may or may not have the force of law, and so on. All of these have to be understood and complied with.

In his book *Using the Law for Competitive Advantage*, George Siedel argues that companies that move swiftly into a state of compliance with new laws tend to gain competitive advantage over those that do not. Early compliance usually involves lower compliance costs, says Siedel, because compliance can be planned and implemented properly rather than in a last-minute rush. Early compliers are thus in a position to move ahead while late compliers must stop and deal with the implications of the new law. Early compliers also gain in reputation terms with governments and regulators; and if they use corporate communications to tell their stories, they can gain in reputation with other stakeholders too.[4]

Figure 8.7 shows the kinds of compliance tasks that need to be undertaken. Managers who merely state that their priority is to 'be compliant' are putting themselves and the company at risk. This is just not good enough. As Figure 8.7 shows clearly, there are many issues that need to be dealt with, many of them in a proactive manner. Nor is compliance simply a matter for 'compliance officers'. At all levels of the organization, both line and functional managers have a duty to ensure compliance on the part of themselves and their staff.

Towards performance excellence

Drivers	Present	Objectives and measures		
	'11E	'12F	'13F	'11F

Legal framework
• Keep informed about legislation and regulatory environment

Corporate structure
• Corporate legal structure in place

• Governance in place

• Brand protection in place

Legal risk management
• Transaction management

• Documentation management/ implementation of email filing policy with support of IT

• Dispute resolution

Objectives and measures

• Attend to new legislation and regulations and increase awareness thereof within the organization by utilization of intranet

• Improve regulatory management by early involvement in regulatory matters, appropriate incident handling and regular communication with regulators

• Ensure preferred structure for legal entities and joint ventures in compliance with local and corp. standards with accurate registration on intranet/cosmos

• Promote good corporate governance practices and enforcement of the Regional Governance Manual

• Manage reputation risk by monitoring surveillance of the brand

• Ensure timely involvement of legal (external/internal) in main legal matters, strategic initiatives and important transactions and improve the quality of legal services in a cost efficient way

• Secure filing and appropriate storage of documentation

• Promote early engagement of legal to prevent litigation and assist in the resolution of disputes to protect the interests of the company

Legal Excellence
○○●●●

FIGURE 8.6 Legal affairs

Towards performance excellence

Regional objectives. Please update status of your business unit

Port / Mkt / Org / Ops / Rep / Fin / Perf

Drivers	Present '06F	Measures '07F	'08F	'09F
Compliance chart and compliance monitoring template	Establish local compliance standards	• Complete local compliance chart and compliance monitoring templates • Enhance compliance requirements on compliance charts, compliance risk mitigation and monitoring • Active use of compliance TPEX for communication with RO		
Risk identification, mitigation and monitoring	Continuous compliance risk identification and assessment of selected BUs Active monitoring of resolution of findings	• Compliance monitor plan/visits at HQ/branch level • Give advices and share best practices with HQ/branch management • Produce compliance monitoring report and capture compliance raised findings/actions in AO scan		
Incident management	Compliance incidents to be included in IR scan Create lessons learnt for compliance incidents Report critical compliance and regulatory issues	• Active use of IR scan to report critical incidents to HO and RO • Create lesson learnt case for training purpose • Timely report all critical compliance and regulatory issues to management and regional compliance • Continuous production of quality compliance reports to management and regional compliance		
Training and education	More trainings to employees and agents	• Training plans to be implemented; e.g. induction course, re-fresher courses, e-learning, case studies to employees and agents, newsletters, etc ...		
Action tracking	Use of AO scan	• Continous active follow up of overdue compliance items • Full implementation of AO scan action tracking system to monitor findings/actions raised by compliance and compliance related actions (raised by CAS, regulators and external auditors) to be followed up by compliance team		
Adviser	Be part of business management and actively participate in ORC/compliance committee	• Compliance provides continuous advice to management • Timely report of critical compliance incidents and findings to management and regional compliance		
Scorecard	Meet the compliance scorecard targets	• Meet minimum 70% 2007 compliance scorecard requirements		
Policies	Fully implement ING group compliance policy and FEC policy Implement new policies/regulations as required	• Rectify identified compliance deficiencies and implement remaining 20% ING compliance policy in 2007 • FIRCOSOFT implementation and existing customers due diligence of FEC policy to be carried out in 2007 and 2008 • implement new policies/regulations as required		

Compliance excellence

FIGURE 8.7 Compliance

BOX 8.2 CONNECTING THE DOTS . . .

How reputation drivers impact on other drivers and vice versa

Portfolio drivers: As noted above, the various sub-drivers of the reputation driver play a key role in achieving strategic success. For instance if a company is seeking to grow organically, it will struggle to expand into new markets unless it can quickly establish its brand and solid reputation there, as we saw in the case of Titan or as ING Direct did in the US. Companies with a good reputation for probity and compliance will also be welcomed by regulators in new markets, whereas those with bad reputations might struggle to get licenses. In the case of M&A, companies with good financial reputations will receive more support from shareholders and financial backers, and those known to be good employers are more likely to be welcomed by employees of the merged or acquired company. Companies with a great global brand and reputation have no problem in entering into partnership with the local 'champions'.

Marketing drivers: Again, reputation impacts directly on brand. Customers will buy products and services they know are reliable and can be trusted. Even a few failures can result in loss of trust and customers withdrawing and turning to other brands. Recent safety issues with some Toyota cars, for example, had a major negative impact on Toyota's global sales.

Organizational drivers: Employees feel that a company's reputation reflects on them. They take pride in working for companies that are liked and trusted, and may feel shame if aspersions are cast on their employer's reputation. This can cause loss of motivation and morale, and just like customers, employees may choose to switch to jobs with other firms, causing a loss of critical skills. Because of its high public reputation, the Tata group is regarded as an employer of choice in India. At BP, on the other hand, morale declined among employees around the world following the bad publicity that resulted from the Gulf of Mexico disaster.

Operational drivers: We saw in the previous chapter how operational problems can affect reputation, but the reverse is true too. If a company has a strong reputation and then suffers problems with its operations, stakeholders are more likely to trust the reputation, at least for a time.

When Tata Motors launched its first road car, the India, in the 1990s, the first models suffered a series of mechanical problems. Customers stayed with the brand, however, because they trusted Tata to put the problem right. On the other hand if a company already has a bad reputation, then even minor defects are highlighted and help to make that bad reputation still worse.

Financial drivers: A reputation for financial solidity, soundness, trust, honesty and probity is vital for any company, but especially for publicly owned ones. They are all summed up in one critical word: confidence. Nothing is more likely to trigger shareholder flight than even a hint of financial irregularity. In finance even more than the rest of the business, companies live and die by their reputations and confidence. Therefore good communications, both short- and long-term, with banks, creditors, ratings agencies, investors and regulators, are of crucial importance.

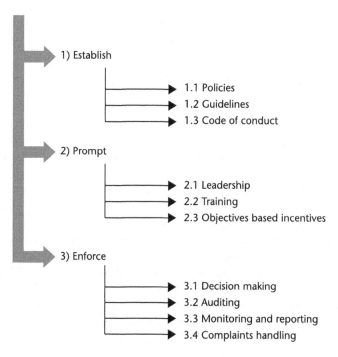

1) Establish
- 1.1 Policies
- 1.2 Guidelines
- 1.3 Code of conduct

2) Prompt
- 2.1 Leadership
- 2.2 Training
- 2.3 Objectives based incentives

3) Enforce
- 3.1 Decision making
- 3.2 Auditing
- 3.3 Monitoring and reporting
- 3.4 Complaints handling

FIGURE 8.8 Integrity management

Connecting the reputation dimension

In recent years reputation and compliance management has developed beyond being a reactive and rather static mitigation activity for correcting or minimizing negative effects from ethics breaches or other managerial misconducts. Today, leading firms deploy reputation and compliance management approaches that proactively influence organizational core processes and employee behaviours. There are two main reason why this holistic view is important: increased pressures from outside of the firm to become better corporate citizens, and from within the firm, driven by more educated and diverse employees especially from generations 'X' and 'Y'. Both trends are reactions to the many publicized cases of company misconduct such as corruption, accounting fraud (e.g. Enron or Lehman Brothers), and human rights violations (e.g. Shell) in the recent past.

Unethical conduct should not just be viewed as lack of integrity or lack of certain character qualities of some individual employees. Such a perspective does not recognize the complexity of most corporate integrity or compliance issues. Research has shown that the apparent frequency of ethical misconduct is being caused by organizational factors including corporate cultures that create enormous psychological pressures on individuals.[5] This then leads to situations where even managers who are considered highly moral deviate from everyday ethical norms. Even more importantly, structural causes are typically the driving forces behind systemic misconduct. These include unbalanced incentive systems that determine bonuses, salary increases or career progression without any consideration of moral behaviour; a lack of responsible leadership; or a climate in which speaking up is not an accepted practice but instead represents a career risk that could lead to repercussions.

Jennings uncovered some of the reasons for the collapse of companies based on ethics issues in her book *Solutions to the Corporate Integrity Quandary.*[6] Companies need to be more proactive in integrating general organizational processes and structural designs rather than being reactive and defensive, solely focused on mitigation and damage control.

The reputation driver has therefore a special role, making sure that not only the 'what' performance question is being answered, but also that the 'how has the performance been achieved?' question is being answered. This perspective assures that integrity management takes reputation beyond compliance towards being a driving force of overall organizational performance.

In addition, effective integrity management is forward looking, beyond philanthropy or charity,[7] in a direction in which social responsibility is perceived as a concept that drives change through economic means. Its processes serve as a platform for disruptive innovation in the social context within a firm's plans to deal with reputation risk, as well as operational and financial risk. The framework's purpose here is to give information about potential risks and where they might come from.

Conclusion

We made the point at the start of this chapter that a company lives and dies by its reputation. Reputational risk is potentially everywhere in the organization, which means that the latent errors that people can make or must be coped with should be part of the management's high priority to manage adequately.

A strong reputation makes it more likely and easier that a business can achieve its strategic goals and achieve performance excellence, while a weak reputation can be a hindrance. But reputations are not created overnight, nor do they grow unaided. Reputations must be monitored and managed.

Nowhere is this more true than in the realm of *finance*, and we will see how this relationship works in the next chapter.

9

THE FINANCIAL DRIVER

This sixth and last driver is concerned with ensuring that all the 'dots' we have looked at under the previous five drivers are also connected with the 'financial dots' of the organization. When we discuss finance, we must be careful not to confuse financial *management* with financial *results*. The latter of course follows from the former; it will be obvious that good results will not be achieved without good management. But good financial management is about more than managing cash-flow or assets or balance sheets. To achieve performance excellence, financial management needs to consider the points listed in Box 9.1. Financial planning, reporting and control, risk management: these are some of the issues on which managers need to focus when considering the financial driver.

BOX 9.1 FINANCIAL DRIVERS

- Control and finance
- Risk management
- Balance sheet management
- Tax planning
- Internal, external reporting

Sharing, aligning and connecting the various elements of the financial driver into the overall management framework enables managers to see the financial consequences of different strategic options. What will be the impact if we spend more on branding, or if we acquire another company? What will be the consequences for our profit and loss account, our balance sheet or even our risk profile? Figure 9.1 shows the financial driver in the lower right hand corner, and indicates how it links to the other five drivers. Financial strategic priorities form an integral part of the organization's total strategic priorities. Figure 9.2 gives an example of what the main strategic financial priorities could look like.

Aspects of the financial driver

Without financial resources, and without solid reporting and control systems to manage those resources, no business will function for very long. The financial driver plays an immensely important role in defining strategy, both in planning and execution. Every initiative has a financial cost and needs funding, and every initiative has − or should have − an intended financial return, taking the form not only of dividends or profits but also of returning the amount invested. Among the tools used to measure return are *return on investment*, *internal rate of return* (IRR) and *pay-back time*. There

Portfolio	Marketing	Organizational
1. Double digit organic growth 2. Active portfolio management (M&A), including better allocation of capital 3. More and stronger partnerships	4. Introduce profitable new product offerings 5. Increase profitable multi-channel sales 6. Develop strategy for youngsters and women 7. Strengthen customer satisfaction	8. Expand organisational capabilities, including management development 9. Improve performance culture
Operational	**Reputation**	**Financial**
10. Increase efficiency and distributor/customer satisfaction 11. Improve operational risk management 12. Obtain/maintain satisfactory audit rating	13. Increase brand recognition 14. Strengthen compliance 15. Communicate clearly to internal/external stakeholders 16. Ensure integrity, ethical behaviour in all areas	17. Raise $ capital + debt 18. Expand value-based management 19. Strengthen risk mgt 20. Improve MIS and control

FIGURE 9.1   Strategic priorities

Towards performance excellence

Illustrative: Please update this slide with strategic priorities for your business unit

Strategic priorities

1. Raise x $ capital and debt
2. Expand value-based management
3. Strengthen risk management
4. Improve MIS and control

FIGURE 9.2 Financial strategic priorities

are also more sophisticated tools such as *value based management* (the economic value a certain initiative is creating) and *risk based returns*, whereby the return is put in the context of the underlying risk. Indeed the higher the expected risk is, the higher the expected return should be.[1] An accurate appraisal of both cost and return is necessary to strategic success.

Yet financial planning and analysis are not a science. Certainties are not on offer; at best there are probabilities, and in many case the actual results will differ markedly from the expected ones. Is this because management or planners have done a bad job? We often hear the question asked when a company runs into trouble: 'Was it bad markets, or bad management?' In fact the managers may be quite competent and may have done their best with the facts or the knowns available to them. The problem is that very often *all* the facts are *not* available. As we saw in Chapter 2, there are many issues that fall into the category of 'known unknowns', issues of which we are aware but do not have precise information, and even more 'unknown unknowns', issues about which we are not aware and therefore can have no knowledge of. All of these combine to ensure that the outcomes we see at the end of the year are often very different from those stated in the plan or the budget.

Take, for example, how simple matters such as a few points of fluctuation either way in interest rates or foreign exchange rates can have a huge impact on revenues and profits. Or consider how the activities of competitors can reduce the certainties of planning to uncertainties in reality. In 2009, Nokia was confident of its position as the market leader in mobile phones. Then along came Apple's iPhone, and suddenly Nokia's position as market leader was under threat. All planning, but especially financial planning, needs to consider how these 'surprises' might impact on the company, and be robust enough to withstand shocks. Remember the adage that 'sticking to the plan could kill your business'.

Recent history is full of cases where companies got their valuations wrong, or miscalculated their expected cash flow, or overestimated their expected revenues. One contributory factor to so many M&As going wrong is that companies overestimate the returns to be yielded from the expected synergy between the two organizations after merging. At the same time, they also underestimate the costs of integration after the merger. We now have an array of very sophisticated tools to model situations and help us make these calculations, yet all too often companies still get them wrong.

Models are useful tools, but they can only take us so far. Models are very good at predicting outcomes in *closed systems*, i.e. situations where all the variables are known and can be predicted. But as we have seen throughout this book, that is not the case in business. We are constantly encountering the unknown and the unexpected, which means we have to face different outcomes from those we planned for. Economic models based on rational expectations and behaviour always run into problems once human behaviour is factored in. Plans based on naive (but feel-good) straight line principles such as 'let's aim for 10 per cent sales growth' are always interrupted by unforeseen cycles and irrational behaviour. Businesses operate in *open systems* whereby it is not possible to account for or predict all the variables.

We need to realize first of all that there are strong limits to our ability to know and to predict. Rather than setting firm targets, managers would do better to establish notional financial targets and then apply frequent reality checks, adjusting their growth targets to the most recent perceived realities. This does not mean managers should not be ambitious. But ambition has to be scaled to reality. What if the sector in which you operate is experiencing flat growth? A target of 10 per cent increase in growth might not be quite so realistic. Even if it is, how can you then be sure you have the capabilities needed to continuously outperform the competition, who will also have their own growth targets? Only by executing frequent reality checks and constant adaptation to the most recent insights and understanding of what is really going on can managers avoid – or at least reduce – the risk of trying to execute on an out-of-date plan.

Some companies try to deal with this problem by applying a 'compass' which tries to adjust for the cyclical factors that they might otherwise overlook. The methodology for adjusting for cyclicality was developed by Professor Robert Shiller at Yale University, who developed methods of better understanding whether markets are 'exaggerating on the upside' or 'exaggerating on the downside'.[2] Shiller developed the 'cyclically-adjusted price/earnings ratio' (CAPE), which notion could also help investors and managers pay more attention to whether we are in an (over) optimistic or (over) pessimistic phase of the economic cycle. This concept is being used increasingly by investors to help them determine where the markets are positioned in the current cycle. Tools like CAPE can help us to avoid falling into the trap of trying to extrapolate the future from historical data (which is what so many planners do).

Therefore, the issues covered by the financial driver require managers to gather as much information as possible in order to reduce complexities and uncertainties. Very often the company already has information that will help to 'make the invisible visible' so far as the finance department is concerned. Market intelligence reports, data from suppliers, information about staff competencies and training requirements, assessments of staff turnover, various risk profiles and beyond these a broader appreciation of where and how top management intends to grow (or downsize) the company can all help financial managers plan more effectively. In order to access this information, however, they must first break out of their own functional silos and reach out to connect the 'dots' right across the company.

BOX 9.2 UNFOUNDED PANIC AND UNEXPECTED DISASTERS

A desire to predict the future is an ancient human trait, but we are not very good at it. Why? First, because the world is too complicated for us to account for every eventuality. Second, because, being social beings, we tend to mirror those around us. Dissidents have few friends. Third, because, being uncertain, we rely on those who we think know best. In ancient times, those were the interpreters of portents. These days, it tends to be economists, academics and celebrities. If all these clever people believe something, who are we to gainsay them? Bernard Madoff

> knew what he was doing when he persuaded the famous to trust him with their money. Fourth, we like stories. We adopt narratives that explain the world and cling to those stories even when the facts suggest they may be wrong. Only when confronted with collapse do we begin to doubt them.
>
> (Michael Shapinker, *Financial Times*, 23 December 2008)

Removing silos

The increasing sophistication and complexities of financial management have raised another problem. No department is more prone to locking itself inside a silo than the finance department. Increasingly, it seems, finance departments are full of finance specialists who so far as the rest of the company is concerned talk a language of their own. In his book *Reinventing the CFO*, Jeremy Hope wrote of how finance departments are becoming increasingly disconnected from the rest of their own firms. Financial managers were becoming increasingly paranoid, feeling that the rest of the organization did not like them and did not understand them. And all too often this was true. People were suspicious about what went on beyond the closed doors of the finance department, and suspicions were exacerbated by the fact that finance directors often enjoy high prestige, sometimes being paid even more than the CEO. Finance professionals, aware of their isolation, were becoming depressed and demotivated. According to Hope, at the time he was writing more than 30 per cent of senior finance professionals were actively considering leaving the profession and retiring. There is no reason to think that this situation has improved today.[3] As a result, finance departments are losing senior and experienced people, at exactly a moment in the economic cycle when they are most needed.

It is therefore essential that we get finance departments back on track and re-integrated into the rest of the business. Finance is so utterly important that it is everyone's business. Specialist professionals are needed to make sense of and interpret complex financial data, but their reports not only need to be shared across the company but should also capture data and information as available and originated in the business units and functional departments. One of Hope's recommendations is that financial reporting should be simplified so that all can understand it easily, and that these simplified reports should be available to every department and business unit so that it is possible for managers to see at a glance the specifics of what is happening. Most managers and companies would agree with this concept in theory. But few can implement it because of lack of the easily accessible and overarching frameworks and templates to get to the specific insights one needs to do so. This is especially true for the activities and plans outside the 'financial spreadsheets'. The need for an overarching management framework with all driver-specific templates will have become increasingly evident to the reader as we progress in this book. Here, we see the need for integrated thinking and reporting driven home.[4]

BOX 9.3 CONNECTING THE DOTS . . .

How financial drivers impact on other drivers and vice versa

Portfolio drivers: Take a planned acquisition as an example. If the target and amount to be paid for the acquisition are known, then the financial consequences in terms of profit and loss and balance sheet should be considered. Also, what will this acquisition mean for the company's profile in terms of rating and cost of borrowing? Alternatively, if the strategy is to grow organically, then the need for working capital might increase. When selling a business unit, the company might receive extra cash to repay outstanding debt or finance another acquisition.

Marketing drivers: Decisions concerning products or channels might have an impact on the cost/income ratios or on the overall profitability of the company. Have all direct and indirect costs and related risk been properly priced? What are the expected returns and values being created? How could we increase the sales per customer or per shop? Solid financial reporting and control will connect a lot of the dots in the marketing area.

Organization drivers: If management decides to strengthen control and risk management, then we need to know how this impacts on drivers like recruitment, training and management development. What numbers and timelines is the CFO thinking of? Sharing these between HR and Finance will connect issues which are not otherwise transparent or accessible to both parties.

Operational drivers: The introduction of a new product, for example, will present issues relating to component sourcing and manufacturing.

The financial consequences such as cost of purchasing, the need to hedge the price risk, supplier credits and so on also need to be taken into account.

Reputation drivers: Good financial management and transparency contributes to reputation.

If a company runs into financial problems, its reputation as a solid and credible counter party or employer is at risk. Misreporting its results or financial position, as happened with Enron and Madoff, can easily lead to a catastrophic loss of reputation. In today's world there are plenty of eyes waiting to scrutinize a company's accounts and financial reports, and pounce on any mistake. Good financial management and good reputation management are closely linked.

Managing finances and financial information

The financial driver of the management framework needs to cover two separate related issues, the management of financial assets and liabilities themselves, including traditional corporate finance functions such as treasury and M&A, but also the control risk, audits and dissemination of financial information. Both are equally vital. The first makes it possible for the company to operate by providing financial resources where and when they are needed and also by monitoring revenue and returning profits to shareholders so as to meet their needs. Managers also have responsibility for managing surplus cash by investing it, safely and yet with good returns. At large international companies this is done by specialists focusing on international cash management, netting surplus balances in one country or business unit with shortfalls in other units. This will also reduce foreign exchange risk and interest costs. The second function, financial reporting and control, makes it possible for the company to understand its present situation, to anticipate and to plan. One of the first questions asked when considering a strategic option, new initiatives or contemplating investments should be: Can we afford it? The framework needs to make certain that the answers to these questions are reliable, quick and easy to understand.

Another important task of finance is control. Big companies have hundreds of controllers and internal auditors to verify whether reporting is done properly, but even very small ones generally have one or more people associated with this function. These managers check whether the reporting and audit standards are being adhered to, and also calculate whether the various strategic initiatives ongoing or proposed are adding value for the company. In recent years there has been a huge growth in the number of of reporting requirements and standards to be met. Some of these have been imposed by governments, others by industry bodies and other independent regulators. The spiralling increase in the levels of supervision and control required is making already complex issues even more complex. On the one hand managers seek to reduce costs, but on the other hand they must spend more to meet these new reporting and control standards. They are also coping with more controllers, fast increase in reporting and audits. This is a paradox which cannot be easily solved, and the net result is that companies are being forced to accept more control which has implications not just for cost but for efficiency and flexibility. Additionally, companies are finding it harder and harder to be fully compliant.

To take one example, a review in the UK by accounting firm Grant Thornton found that just 51 per cent of FTSE 350 companies were fully compliant with the requirements of the UK's corporate governance code. However, only 16 per cent provided enough disclosure to support whether they were compliant or not. And only 112 of the 350 companies provided general risk descriptions or explained how they managed risk.[5] Do companies not want to disclose how effective they are at corporate governance? This seems unlikely. Much more likely is the case that lack of fully aligned management and information processes to transmit information means that these companies do not really know themselves whether they are compliant. Only with a fully integrated management framework, transmitting information about 'what, how and who' issues, will they ever really know for certain.

Priorities within the financial driver

After having defined the financial strategic priorities by management together with the financial managers, the next step is to determine and list the relevant specifics. The following sub-drivers need to be considered:

tax planning and reporting;
external reporting, such as:
    investors, analysts, banks, bond holders and media,
    regulators, supervisors, SOX reporting;
efficiency improvement programmes: improve cost/income ratio, better
    management of capital, etc.;

performance analysis of specific business units or departments: should some be 'fixed or exited'? If so this should be reported under the port-folio driver (see Chapter 4).

Let us see how this might work when 'cascading down' the four priorities in Figure 9.2.

Raising capital and balance sheet management

There are few activities or initiatives within a business that do not have an impact on the financial position of a company, or at least of individual busi-ness units within a company. The interdependencies between actions and money need to be made visible. Most companies already collect the rele-vant data through financial reporting systems. Yet frequently the data gathered are presented in a way that is inconsistent, incomplete and un-comprehensive; in other words, not compliant with the concept of the 3Cs. By aligning and embedding financial reporting into the planning process and at all layers of the organization, the company will get relevant data about how much internal and external cash it needs for financing its growth and all related initiatives. Considering that most companies are the sum of a group of companies/business units with different situations, it is important that each unit reports its specific needs.

Let us take an example. The VW business unit might decide to go to the financial market to raise $1 billion to finance a combination of planned organic growth and a planned acquisition. Yet the Audi business unit (also part of VW Group) might be in a different position. It may be planning to finance its own growth from excess cash and internal cash flow. The Audi unit might therefore set as a financial objective 'improve the risk/return ratio of their excess cash' or 'return excess cash to VW Group'.

Relevant questions concerning balance sheet management could include:

1. How much capital do we need to finance all the initiatives as described in the plan?
2. How much is required for organic growth and how much for acquisi-tions (minus exits, sell-offs)?
3. How much will come from internally generated cash flows (profit/depreciation)?
4. How much is needed for working capital?
5. How will funding be raised: in the form of equity, forms of debt, internal cash flows?

6.   What is the cost of capital?
7.   What is the outlook of the various rating agencies, and what impact will this have on on cost of capital?
8.   What are the solvency and liquidity ratios?
9.   What are the counter-party risks: customer credits, risk from banks, supplier risk?
10. How will we manage relationships with investors, banks, creditors?
11. What reporting and compliance requirements must we meet?

Depending on the size and ownership profile (whether publicly or privately owned) it could be good to 'check' at least some of these questions, and very likely all of them.

Value-based management

Many companies judge the performance of their business units or investment plans by looking at the profit as reported by the unit or in the investment plan. But how much risk is involved? Or how much value (next to profit) is being created or destroyed? High-risk plans require a larger capital allocation than do low-risk ones. Both the costs of an initiative and the economic value it will add to the company need to be considered as part of value-based management. As an example, upgrading call centres to make them more responsive to customer needs will cost money. It could be argued that these costs will only result in value in the long run; alternatively, it could also be that customer satisfaction scores will rise as a result of this upgrade, which will improve the cross-sell ratio and future profits. This too means economic value creation for the company.

Improving risk management

Risk can have a number of different dimensions. Banks, for example, typically look at risk related to their loans to borrowers. If their borrowers are based in other countries, the banks are also exposed to country risk. Non-financial sector companies incur similar risks when doing business with their customers. Companies might also incur risks relating to operations, or legal risks. If the balance sheet is not adequately financed, the company might be exposed to liquidity risk or in other words become short of cash.

By mapping or listing the various categories of risk (see Figure 9.3) as part of the framework, the company makes sure that all business units are

Towards performance excellence →

Objectives and measures

Driver	Present ('10E)	'11F	'12F	'13F

– Implement risk mgt framework
 	
– Control risk categories
  1. Counter party risk
  2. Country risk
  3. Operational risk
	Ensure IRM reporting processes are auditable
	Develop and Test
	Training and communication
	No deficiencies
		• Pass audit of cash flow generation and input into ECAPS in Q1/Q2 2007, including auditable MCEV and EC figures with a satisfactory rating or higher, maintain this level ongoing, to be audited annually.
		
		• Agree architecture for automated data feeds to ECAPS by Q2 2007.		

Embed EC and managing for value • Prepare and train management for the new metrics (MCEV)	SoP compliance Add value Efficient product review process	• Integration with MIS/decision making. • Removal of all significant and notable SOX deficiencies. • IRisk area needs to become an integral value added part of the product development process in 2007. New sales IRR minimum in WACC + 3.5%.		
• Application in pricing (MCEV(0)) • Balance value via returns / volumes	Completely switch to MCEV during 2007 MCEV(0) in PARP To include value in KPI	• Control/reduce the turn around time of product review. • MCEV documentation and methodology, and implement MCEV. • All products including revisions must have MCEV(0) calculated and documented by EOY 2007, MCEV(0) should be documented in the PARP for approval. • To include VNS and EVP in the KPIs of business unit.		
People • Recruit more specialists • Train for broader risk management	Recruit 5 risk managers 2 analysts.	• Talent assessment of the insurance risk teams in early 2007. • Appropriate training and investment. • Turning actuaries into risk professionals. • Improve / increase bench strength across network and recognition of high performers.		
Enhance Performance Culture • Effective communication • Quality reporting to standards • 360-feedback mechanism	Train 3 specialists externally Excellence in our daily jobs Value added analysis 360 reviews in place	• Risk and actuarial reporting. • Focus on value added analysis and decision. • Improve interface with investment area: ALCO, investment mandates. • 360 reviews for the CIRO and top level direct reports of the insurance risk team in 2007.		

Risk management excellence
○○○
●●●●

FIGURE 9.3 Risk management

aware of all levels of risk. Otherwise there is a danger that business units might focus just on those risks immediately in front of them (for example, the risks incurred by pushing for more sales) and not on the less visible but equally important risks that surround the company as a whole. It is not just lack of financial risk management that drags companies down, but lack of *total* risk management. As we saw in Chapter 1, BP, a financially well managed company, nevertheless incurred huge financial losses when risks relating to operations were not properly assessed.

Improving MIS reporting and control

Figure 9.4 shows an example of sub-drivers that could be listed when a company wants to improve its MIS reporting and control. Issues such as new reporting formats, or recruiting and training more financial controllers, could be set as priorities. Tax planning is another aspect that is important to include. Specific KPIs can be added by each business unit when applicable. The consequences in terms of costs of these initiatives can be made visible as well.

Conclusion

Every manager at all levels, units and functions must ask themselves the following questions:

- Do we have enough financial resources to carry out our strategy?
- Are our financial insights and controls adequate?
- Do we have sufficient information and resources to understand, monitor and manage risk?

Basically, all decisions as taken or to be taken under the other drivers in the framework have an impact on the 'financials' of the company. By making the main drivers transparent as part of the total process of working towards performance excellence, the company should become much more effective and efficient. In Chapter 10 we will look at how that search for performance excellence finally reaches its goal.

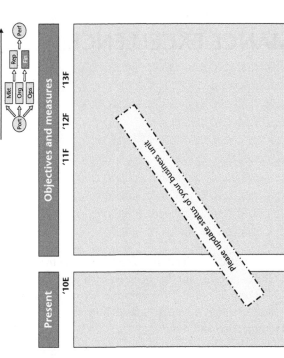

Towards performance excellence

Driver	Present	Objectives and measures

'10E   '11F   '12F   '13F

Please update status of your business unit

Financial control
- Implement SOX (for SOX units)
- Documented financial control procedures

Financial reporting and analysis
- Detailed source of earnings
- Business analysis

Financial systems and database mgt.
- Financial database with detail information

Capital Management and tax
- Tax compliance

Expense management
- Implement project expense review

Finance spearheads
- HR
- Communication
- Continous improvement projects

Control finance excellence

FIGURE 9.4 Control and finance

10

PERFORMANCE EXCELLENCE

Chapters 2 and 3 of this book explained the overall rationale for management frameworks. Chapters 4 through 9 explained each of the six drivers of performance excellence in detail, dealing with the 'what, how and who' questions. In this short chapter we shall look at how the process pulls together and leads to outcomes and results.

To put it very simply: *vision + action = result!*

The result must of course be measured against the original mission and stated objectives. If the company's original goal was 'to become the customer's preferred choice', we might want to measure the outcome by looking at customer satisfaction (or dissatisfaction) scores and whether the company gained market share. If one of our goals was to build value for all stakeholders, we should measure this through qualitative and quantative KPIs such as as shareholder value creation and staff satisfaction scores.

What is the best way to set and measure results? Basically, this should be done using two sets of measures:

1. *Quantitative* objectives and measures, such as sales, net profits, etc.
2. *Qualitative* objectives and measures, such as improvements in risk management, customer satisfaction, employee commitment, etc.

Below you will find two templates that show how to get to an effective overview of the measures an organization wants to use to measure outcomes or results. One template (Figure 10.1) lists a series of quantitative measures of performance. The other (Figure 10.2) lists qualitative measures grouped according to our six drivers, showing how a combination of scores can be used to score overall corporate performance.

In the spreadsheet shown in Figure 10.1 each business unit will report its numbers such as gross and net sales, profits, cash flow and so on. Managers are also asked to discuss the performance of their business unit, explaining how the numbers should be understood and the reasons that lie behind the reported performance. Actual numbers will be compared with the budget, and major deviations will be discussed and explained. If necessary, updated forecasts of the numbers can be added. Management can also share ideas on measures to achieve further improvement in the results. Some of the numbers generated thus (net sales, EBIT, dividends) can be used for bonus setting as part of the quantitative goals and measures, as shown in Figure 10.2.

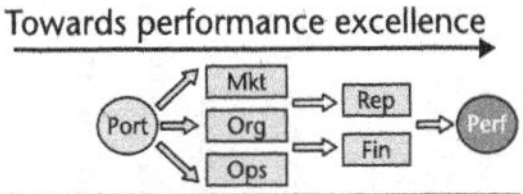

Towards performance excellence

EUR million	2010F	2011F	2012F	2013F	2014F	
Gross revenues						
Net revenues						
Cost of sales						
Profit contribution						
Operational cost						
Purchasing cost						
Staff cost						
Depreciation						
Value of new business						
Cost/income ratio						
Cash flow						
Market value at risk						
Economic capital						
vROEC						
Capital, funding needed						
Dividends						
Audit scores						

Performance excellence

FIGURE 10.1   Quantitative performance

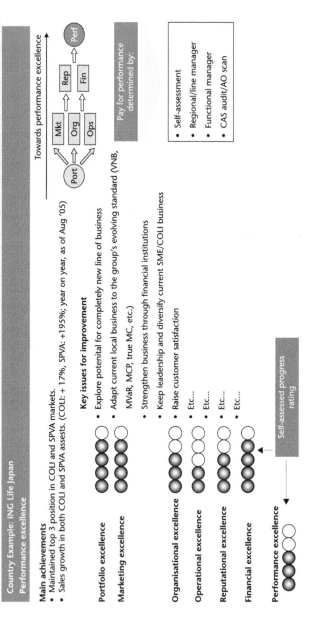

FIGURE 10.2 Qualitative performance

In addition to the quantitative goals and results, an organizition should be led and managed by qualitative goals and results. These qualitative goals can be guided by the strategic objectives as listed under the six drivers in Figure 3.5. It will have been noticed that in Chapters 4–9, each template shown has a series of five circles at the bottom. The purpose of these is to measure progress towards qualitative goals on a scale of 1–5. When no circles are coloured in, or only one or two, then progress is still required. Three can be considered an average score, while four or five indicates good progress is being made.

If a similar approach is followed with all six drivers, this will result in a set of comparable scores which measures *overall* performance towards targets (though looking at areas with low scores will also help to highlight areas where more work is needed). These qualitative scores, taken together with the quantitative results, mean we can measure the overall performance of each business unit. The final step is to add up all the scores of all the business units (including staff departments) in order to get a reasonably objective and transparent view of how the entire organization is performing. For determining the actual scores, the following inputs will be needed:

1. self-assessment by managers themselves;
2. assessment by their respective line manager(s);
3. assessment by their respective functional manager(s);
4. information from the auditors, based on audit reports.

Figure 10.2 is an example of how the *quantitative* and *qualitative* objectives can be set and measured. Obviously different targets can be set on individual basis; these are examples only.

Any actual score of five would mean the manager has scored the highest mark available and his or her unit has performed at or above the profit goal as set in the plan. Similarly if the qualitative score for the reputational driver is a 3, it could mean that some of the targets have not been achieved.

The use of standardized templates across the company means that all objectives and KPIs can be aligned and compared to give us a total picture, while still giving us the flexibility to 'zoom in' and concentrate on a few parts of the company as needed, in order to look at individual performance within the broader context. Senior managers, auditors and controllers can thus see easily and clearly which departments and business units are performing well and which units need to improve.

The old adage that 'what gets measured, gets done', can be restated as 'what gets *listed* and measured, gets done . . . and paid for'. By defining and listing the desired objectives and outcomes at all levels and departments in the entire organization, an organization will be able to create a well aligned process to help it achieve performance excellence. The overarching management framework thus becomes a very effective planning and execution tool for management at all layers to achieve objectives.

When people discuss performance, more fairness will be introduced in the discussion when there is a distinction between performance that is *externally* determined and performance that consists of *internally* driven results. Or as mentioned in Chapter 9, but now in the positive sense, if results are good, is this because of excellent management and/or because of favourable markets? Obviously many results are not necessarily the results of great strategies of or execution by *existing* management. When judging performances, remuneration committees and boards are well advised to consider whether certain outcomes are to be credited to present management and thus not due or thanks to previous management's actions and/or external factors.

However, a word of caution is in order on the subject of performance-linked pay. Discussions about bonuses have been prominent in the news over the past few years and questions have been asked about fairness and proportionality. After the financial crisis began in 2007 many people began to wonder how those responsible for the major losses were still getting big bonuses. For example how could Kraft's CEO, Irene Rosenfeld, get a bonus of $2.1 million while missing her financial targets? The explanation, that she was responsible for 'improved talent pipeline' and 'improved year on year diversity representation', is as mind-boggling for Kraft insiders as it is for outsiders.[1]

Competition analysis

'The best source of inspiration is irritation'

Many managers get a feeling of irritation when they see that their competitor is doing better than their business unit. This can be the best source of inspiration. It can lead to the need to search for ways to improve as well or to catch up or speed up or even to outperform their rivals. Thanks to Japan or Germany having several car manufacturers, these have been more successful than they might have been were there only one car producer per country. Competition drives innovation and better performance.

Most managers analyse and benchmark their company's (and thus their own) performance mostly by looking at *what* the competitor has achieved such as growth in sales and how they are positioned on the various rankings. Rarely do they study and analyse *how* their competitors are achieving their performance. When ING Asia Pacific was researching their main rivals in 2006, they focused more on the 'how' than on the 'what' question. They tried to get as much information as possible and 'plotted' this in each step of their management framework. If the most successful competitor had much higher sales or profits, could it be that the real 'reason behind the reason' was that they had a different vision, mission, strategy, or different strategic priorities and/or a better way of executing them? Can the templates of a management framework be used to map competitor strategy as well as one's own?

The answer is 'yes', provided one has access to informaton about that company. We show here (Figures 10.3 and 10.4) how the portfolio and marketing templates might look when one is analysing a competitor company using the key sub-drivers.

Similar analysis can be done by gathering data on the other four drivers, as well as for the overall performance excellence data, such as financial data. An overview is then created which shows the areas where the company can learn from the better or best practices of their competing firms. This in turn could result in adapting certain strategies and priorities, or adding new ways of working, or redesigning or repricing certain products. By improving in this fashion, it should be possible to outperform those competitors.

Be careful when comparing rankings

Senior management, boards, supervisors or even analysts might want to bear in mind the following possible 'pitfalls' when management presents them with certain rankings or graphs:

(a) When comparing rankings or graphs, ensure you know what is being compared: are they 'like for like' rankings?

(b) Beware of bias: for example, one could 'cherry pick' certain rankings which are or look more favourable to us. The rankings might exclude bad rankings like a low score on customer satisfaction. Sometimes

Vision/mission	• Superior shareholder returns through relentless focus on top line growth and tight expense control • Diversity of business lines, geography and distribution channel provides stability
Strategic direction	• Early market penetration where possible • Maximize all distribution channels (drive multiple distribution) • Achieve critical mass and market dominance
Business portfolio management	• Japan reports directly to home office because of its size • Multiple parallel businesses in Asia allows concentration on product/distribution and lower head to head channel conflict • Life insurance for Asia ex Japan headquartered in Hong Kong • Countries divided into mature businesses (e.g. Hong Kong, Taiwan, Philippines) and emerging businesses (e.g. China, India, Vietnam)
SWOT	**Strengths** • Critical mass and dominant position • Early market entry into key emerging markets of India and China • Highly disciplined, focused management team with clear processes that are easily leveraged **Weaknesses** • Unbending corporate culture does not encourage internal dissent or divergence • Dependence on agency model with related high margin products in mist markets despite efforts to build multiple channel distribution **Opportunities** • Blue sky growth opportunities in emerging markets • Huge growth potential in Japan vs 5 largest local competitors • Maintain dominance and extract margin on other countries **Threats** • Emergence of alternative distribution • Challenging dependency on agency • Regulatory pressures including product transparency, accountability for advice, etc.

FIGURE 10.3 Competition portfolio analysis

Customer

- Corporate focuses on customer management not well translated into Asian business operations
- Business remains predominantly sales-focused with dominant agency channels self selecting own customer management process

Product

- Products priced for maximum profitability; x is able to leverage strong brand, non-competitive distribution and superior S&P rating to achieve and maintain high margins and superior profitability
- Rigid controls on pricing (little freedom at a country level to set own pricing); volume/scale; cost controls and leverage of IT platforms contribute to reputation for best margin and lowest expense ratio of any company
- Over recent years numerous product development initatives have taken place which indicate centralized control is not impeding efficiency. Examples include Syriah compliant products in Indonesia, Unversal Life in Korea and Thailand, family-based accident and health cover in India, and unit linked and single premium products in HK and Singapore
- Countries divided into mature businesses (e.g. Hong Kong, Taiwan, Philippines) and emerging businesses (e.g. China, India, Vietnam)

Sales and distribution

- Agency model highly developed, very efficient and easily replicated into new markets
- Pressure in some markets from overly dominant agency leaders causing the company to find strategies to go around these blockages
- Numerous attempts at alternative strategies but few have "stuck". If an option is not working, it is closed down very quickly
- Company recognizes the need to develop alternative distribution (especially bancassurance) however has found practical difficulties doing so as management skills and experience favour agency
- Japan is an exception, with three different companies each specializing in their own business lines and distribution
- Typical x model relies on high margin products and requires a market with low levels of transparency, consumer sophistication and regulatory intrusion. This is a potential threat to the continuation of the business model in the medium/long term

FIGURE 10.4 Competition marketing analysis

management might share with you data indicating that they are well positioned regarding sales performance, but not share the data showing that they are badly ranked regarding customer services and profitability.

(c) Are there different sources of similar rankings? Think about which rankings the competitor would show to their management and how would we rank on those lists? For example you can advance a lot if you change the currency or take different periods or definitions.

(d) Moving upwards faster than the industry average is easier than being ahead of your most respected rivals. The UK soccer club Manchester United might move up from fourth place to third in the Premier League, but if their real goal was to become number one, then their fans might be quite disappointed.

(e) As mentioned and argued above, what should be measured and compared is not only the final result, but more importantly the reasons behind why the scores are as they are. As argued before (and excluding external factors), the ultimate performance is the result of the quality of the total process in getting alignment in strategy, execution and organization. How do we score as compared to our main rivals (not the industry average!) on the various drivers to get to performance excellence? Companies don't go as far and deep as sports clubs do. Sports coaches don't merely look at the results of the games (comparable to managers looking at their financial figures) and the weekly rankings, which most business managers do only once a year. Professional coaches research how many times player X received or shot the ball correctly and exactly how he or she did that, and so on. This more detailed analysis is what gives clubs and organizations the cutting edge: a more profound analysis of the data is needed if they are to excel.

Conclusion

As the saying goes, predicting the future is not what it used to be. The same is true when it comes to measuring achievements and outcomes. Daniel Kahneman, who won the Nobel Prize for economics in 2002 for his work on decision-making and uncertainty, has argued that even if you have perfect foreknowledge and a CEO with brilliant vision and extraordinary competence, you will still be unable to predict how the company will perform with much more accuracy than the flip of a coin.

However, by applying the planning and execution process we described in previous chapters, on a consistent, complete and comprehensive (3C) basis, it becomes much easier to measure results against plan. The many objectives and KPIs can be easily summarized to give a broad overview. Moreover, unknown or unexpected events can be responded to more quickly and easily than if the company is wedded to a single planning process. This will leave all stakeholders – and the company itself – better informed and better off.

11

CONNECTING THE DOTS

A unified model for management frameworks

A management framework which is complete, consistent and comprehensive (3C) should help a company to proceed from vision and mission and strategic direction through deployment of resources and strategic execution to reach its targets. The framework should be dynamic, adaptive and capable of continuous improvement. An overarching management framework should also be capable of customization in order to capture the needs of the whole company and also of specific business units. Figure 11.1 shows the required elements.

When looking at Figure 11.1, especially the rectangular grey box, it can be seen that the most important steps are those that follow the path from vision and mission to performance excellence. Yet we still have to review and connect other 'dots' in order to meet the 3C requirement. Though most of the relevant drivers (and their objectives and KPIs) are already part of the grey rectangle, the dynamic management of these drivers is done through the four yellow 'inputs' in the framework. Each of these is now discussed in turn.

Planning, objectives and KPIs

An overarching management framework should have as its main purpose the putting in place of a structured, well aligned process that assists

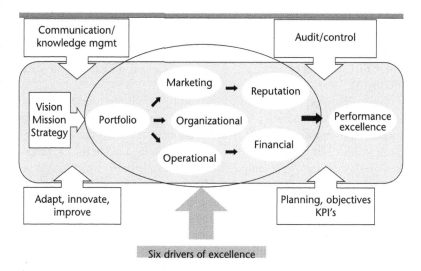

FIGURE 11.1 A comprehensive, complete and consistent set of frameworks

managers in planning and executing strategy. Input and output of data play a key part in the up- and downloading of the various drivers, as discussed in Chapters 4–9. For example, salespeople must input their expected sales numbers per region and per distribution point. They also can draw down the data they need to achieve their goals, such as their cost budget, to support the launching of new products. If these data are all available in a structured, simple and well aligned set of templates, it will be much easier to share these with other stakeholders.

If all data and initiatives are complete, consistent and comprehensive, then it will be much easier to add them up. If for instance twenty business units report the number of staff they wish to see trained over a given period, it will be easier for the regional or global head of HR to add up the numbers and calculate the total impact on cost. This projected cost can then be compared to the overall training budget.

Adapt, innovate and improve

In the words of economist John Kay, 'Large and complex corporations not only are, but could only be, the product of incremental change and adaptation. Businesses are also complex systems. We tend to infer design where there was only adaptation and improvisation.'[1] The limitations of forecasting, budgeting and financial planning were pointed out in Chapter 9. We hope for certainty, but all to often as managers we have to admit that 'we don't know', or 'we are not sure' or 'we now know with hindsight'.

Given the lack of clear and full visibility of what is ahead of them, companies need to have a process and a culture in place which supports continuous improvement and enables them to adapt as as quickly as possible. Flexibility and adaptability should be embedded in the organization and its culture, for example through 'idea factories' which could be the breeding ground for new ideas and innovation. The generation of new ideas is not just the task of R&D, and should take place throughout the organization. If constant adaptation and improvement become part of the culture, this will help the entire organization to look for insights and ideas which might help it to improve performance.

In an interview in *McKinsey Quarterly* in 2007, management guru Gary Hamel shares his view on the twenty-first-century management model and makes the point that decision-making will be more peer-based, the tools of creativity will be widely distributed in organizations, ideas will compete on an equal footing, strategies will be built from the bottom up, and power will be a function of competence rather than position.[2] His view underpins the importance of having processes in place across the entire organization, in which ideas and decisions about the 'what, how and who' issues can constantly and equally move up and down. If this is supported by the 'idea factory' concept outlined above, staffed by empowered creative people to create and support the flow of ideas, the company can keep adapting and reinventing itself, and in an orderly way.

Communication/knowledge management

It is generally believed that more effective communication across the company will allow the sharing of best practices and thus greater effectiveness and efficiency. Communication and knowledge-sharing should take place at all levels and ranks. But how can such communication and sharing take place in a structured and efficient 3C way? Many companies struggle to get this right. Many end up with a knowledge management portal (and a department) which has become a kind of library of all kinds of documents and books people have wanted to share. But documents tend to get dumped into silos – operations, innovation, leadership, etc. – which don't always match people's own needs for information. It makes much more sense to link the communication and knowledge sharing system to the framework used for planning and reporting, and use the same templates. This means that everyone has access to complete, consistent and comprehensive information. ING Asia Pacific's knowledge portal, TPEX, is an example of how this can be done (see Figure 11.2). On TPEX, all relevant knowledge was available through the same logic and systems as used by the company's TPE management framework. For instance, if people wanted information about operations, they would search the operational driver. The respective functional departments were responsible for keeping their 'sites' up to date. The business unit in Japan could easily share and exchange data with colleagues in Hong Kong. The team running the cross-regional operational efficiency projects (see Chapter 7) used the TPEX portal as an effective tool to share information and best practices.

Audit and control

Every organization above a certain size has auditors, people who check on a regular basis whether things are being done as they should be done. Many organizations are also examined by external auditors, regulators, supervisors and inspectors. Most internal and external auditors and controllers look not only at their specific area of responsibility but also at the status and the quality of the total process.

Companies which do not have 3C reporting processes in place, along the lines we have discussed in this book, will have difficulty in demonstrating to auditors and regulators that they are operating efficiently and in compliance with regulations. In consequence, it will be very difficult for the auditors and controllers to confirm that management has well aligned, solid and robust control mechanisms in place. Since most companies *don't* have these in place, they should not qualify for a 'satisfactory' rating. (Nevertheless many do get a satisfactory rating, very often because many auditors and controllers are not aware that there are better ways of 'management of management' of a company. They have not been told about or trained in new and better approaches to management.)

Once the auditors have access to the total process, from the 'big picture framework' to each specific template of what and how things will be done and how they are connected and aligned, supported by simple information about who is responsible for what, they will be much better informed about the quality and the efficiency of the managerial processes. They will

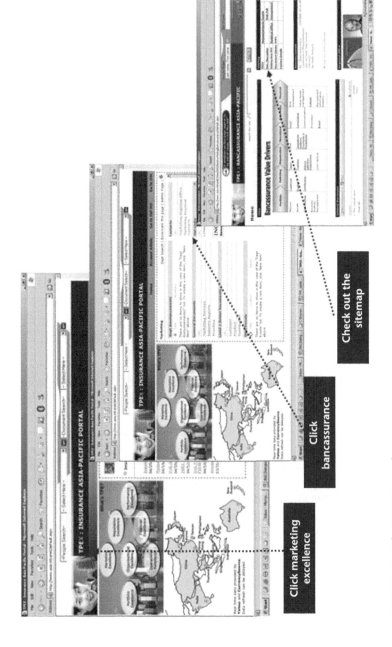

FIGURE 11.2 The TPEX portal

be able to identify potential weaknesses and risks in a much more effective and thorough way than if these 3C processes were not in place.

Aligning the total process with total organization

We have now taken you through the 'total picture' by connecting the lines between the dots in an orderly way. There is still one final step to completion. How do we know that all managers in all business units and departments will be well aligned and sufficiently engaged with 'everything and everybody', thus within the entire organization? As you will remember from Chapters 1–3, one of the key concerns in managing complexity concerns 'bad' management in an organization. When managers at different levels (i.e. head office, business units, regions and functions) are not properly connected or well aligned to each other, or when people are thinking and acting too much in their own silos, then we can assume that there are elements of 'bad management'. In order to address these concerns, the following overarching template shows how an organization can become better connected and aligned at the various levels (see left-hand side of Figure 11.3). These organizational layers will actively drive the three main areas of management's attention: *strategy, execution* and *organization*, or in simple terms: the *what, how* and *who* questions.

Conclusion

We have reached the end of this stage of our journey through the world of improving the 'management of management' through management frameworks. We started by arguing that the complexities of the modern world mean it is no longer possible to manage by ad hoc methods. Frameworks bring an order and discipline to management and make it possible for managers to get a clear picture of what is really going on inside and outside the organization. We showed how frameworks need to be linked to mission, vision and strategy, and should support both the design and execution of strategy; in other words, the framework needs to be designed with the company's strategic needs in mind. Among other things, the framework must be adaptable and able to support the inevitable strategic changes that will come. We then described the six drivers, outlining the importance of each and describing the questions that must be asked and answered. Throughout we have emphasized the interconnectedness of these drivers

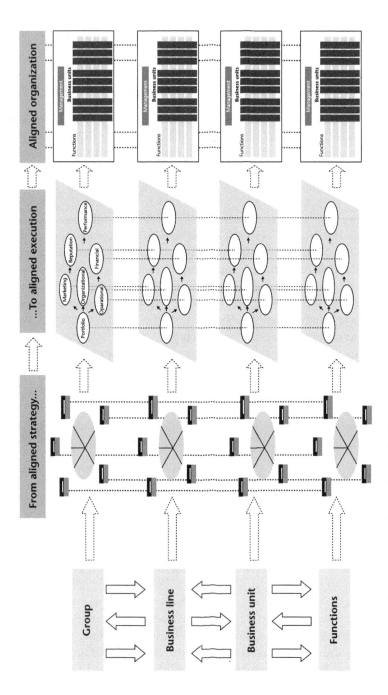

FIGURE 11.3 Strategy, execution and organization

and how each impacts on the others. Finally, we have shown how the framework can be used to monitor progress on plan, and also to monitor and assess competition.

For students of strategy, frameworks are a very useful tool. There is, as we described in Chapter 2, a good deal of literature describing various frameworks. Additionally, the TPE framework that we have alluded to several times is described in more detail in a case study, *Jacques Kemp: Towards Performance Excellence*, published by the Richard Ivey School of Business at the University of Western Ontario. Finally, there is an electronic learning resource, again based on the TPE framework, available from Routledge at www.routledge.com/books/details/9780415781657/. We hope that these and other resources will enable you to better understand the strategic needs of organizations, the interconnected elements of strategy and the need for a conistent, complete and comprehensive approach to the subject. We welcome feedback on any aspect of this book or on the subject more generally, and look forward to assisting your learning on this most vital and fascinating of subjects.

NOTES

1 Too complex to manage?

1 Société Générale's losses are said to be the largest ever suffered by a bank at the hands of a rogue trader; 'Société Générale trader Kerviel jailed for three years', BBC News, 5 October 2010.
2 Peter Chapman, *The Last of the Imperious Rich: Lehman Brothers, 1844–2008*, London: Portfolio, 2010, p. 274.
3 Tom FitzGerald and John Collins, 'The CFO as Corporate Prophet', *Corporate Finance Review*, July–August 2006: 13–18.
4 Eric D. Beinhocker, *The Origin of Wealth: Evolution, Complexity and the Radical Remaking of Economics*, New York: Random House, 2007, p. 6.
5 M. Greto, A. Schotter and M. Teagarden, *Toyota: The Accelerator Crisis*, Thunderbird Case Series. Glendale, AZ: Thunderbird School of Global Management, 2010.
6 Jim Collins and Jerry Porras, *Built to Last: The Successful Habits of Visionary Companies*, New York: HarperBusiness, 1997; Jim Collins, *Good to Great: Why Some Companies Make the Leap . . . And Others Don't*, New York: HarperBusiness, 2001; see also Daniel Kahneman, *Thinking Fast and Slow*, New York: Farrar, Straus and Giroux, 2011.
7 Beinhocker, *The Origin of Wealth*, p. 6.
8 David J. Snowden and Mary E. Boone, 'A Leader's Framework for Decision Making', *Harvard Business Review*, November 2007: 69–76.
9 Herbert Spencer, *Principles of Biology*, 1864, repr. Honolulu: University Press of the Pacific, 1962.
10 From 'The Baseline Scenario', see: http://baselinescenario.com/2010/01/16/too-big-to-regulate/

11 Kurt Richardson, 'Managing Complex Organizations: Complexity Thinking and the Science and Art of Management', *Corporate Finance Review*, 10(2) (2008): 13–26.

12 Alfred D. Chandler, *The Visible Hand: The Managerial Revolution in American Business*, Cambridge, MA: Belknap Press, 1977.

13 Jagdish Sheth, *The Self-Destructive Habits of Good Companies*, Upper Saddle River, NJ: Wharton School Publishing, 2007, p. 215.

14 Charles Handy, *The Empty Raincoat*, London: Arrow, 1995.

15 John Kay, *Obliquity: Why Our Goals Are Best Achieved Indirectly*, London: Profile Books, 2010.

16 Kay, *Obliquity*, p. 44.

17 Kay, *Obliquity*, p. 158.

18 Jeremy Hope and Steve Player, *Beyond Performance Management*, Boston: Harvard Business School Press, 2012.

19 Schotter, A. and Beamish, P. W., 'Performance Effects of MNC Headquarters', *Journal of International Management*, 17(3):243–59.

20 Robert J. Gordon, *The American Business Cycle: Continuity and Change*, Chicago: University of Chicago Press, 1990; Robert J. Shiller, *Irrational Exuberance*, New York: Broadway, 2001.

2 The architecture of an organization

1 Casson, Herbert N., *The Story of My Life*, London: Efficiency Magazine, 1931.

2 Andreas Schotter c.s. 2010/2011.

3 Fayol, Henri (1916) *Administration industrielle et générale*, trans. Irwin Gray, New York: David S. Lake, 1984; Gulick, Luther H., 'Notes on the Theory of Organization', in Luther H. Gulick and Lyndall Urwick (eds), *Papers on the Science of Administration*, New York: Institute for Public Administration, 1937; Taylor, Frederick Winslow, *The Principles of Scientific Management*, New York: Harper & Bros, 1911; Kanigel, Robert, *The One Best Way: Frederick Taylor and the Enigma of Efficiency*, New York: Viking Penguin, 1997.

4 Porter, Michael E., *Competitive Strategy: Techniques for Analyzing Industries and Competitors*, New York: The Free Press, 1980; Ansoff, H. I., *Corporate Strategy*, London: McGraw-Hill, 1965.

5 Kotler, Philip, *Marketing Management*, Engelwood Cliffs, NJ: Prentice-Hall, 9th edn, 1997.

6 Mintzberg, Henry, *Mintzberg on Management*, New York: The Free Press, 1989; Mintzberg, Henry, *The Rise and Fall of Strategic Planning*, New York: The Free Press, 1994.

7 Andersen, M. M., Froholdt, M. and Poulfelt, F., *Return on Strategy: How to Achieve It*, New York: T&F books, 2010.

8 Kaplan, R. S. and Norton, D. P., 'Linking the Balanced Scorecard to Strategy', *California Management Review*, 39(1) (1996): 53–79.

9 Pryor, M. G., White, J. C. and Toombs, L. A., *Strategic Quality Management: A Strategic, Systems Approach to Quality*, Albany, NY: Thomson Learning, 1998.

10 Rasiel, E. and Friga, P. N., *The McKinsey Mind: Understanding and Implementing the Problem-Solving Tools and Management Tech-niques of the World's Top Strategic Consulting Firm*, New York: McGraw-Hill, 2001.

11 Peters, T. and Waterman, R., *In Search of Excellence*, New York and London: Harper & Row, 1982.

12 Ibid.

13 Ibid.

14 www.mindtools.com/pages/article/newSTR_91.htm; accessed 13 February 2011.

15 Pryor, White and Toombs, *Strategic Quality Management*.

16 Pryor, M. G., Anderson, D., Toombs, L. A. and Humphreys, J. H., 'Strategic Implementation as a Core Competency: The 5P's Model', *Journal of Management Research*, 7(1) (2007): 3–17.

17 Ibid.

18 Kaplan, R. and Norton, D., 'The Balanced Scorecard – Measures that Drive Performance', *Harvard Business Review*, 69(1) (1992): 71–79.

19 Kaplan, R. and Norton, D., *The Balanced Scorecard: Translating Strategy into Action*, Boston, MA: Harvard Business School Press, 1996.

20 Kaplan, R. and Norton, D., *The Strategy Focused Organization*, Boston, MA: Harvard Business School Press, 2001.

21 Kaplan and Norton, *The Balanced Scorecard*.

22 Coelho, A. and Purdy, L., *Two Alternative Approaches to the Evaluation of Performance: 360-Degree Feedback and the Balanced Scorecard*, London, Ontario: Ivey Publishing, 2003.

23 Kaplan, R. and Norton, D., 'Having Trouble with Your Strategy? Then Map It', *Harvard Business Review*, 77 (2000): 167–76.

24 Kaplan and Norton, *The Strategy Focused Organization*.

25 Accenture, 'Driving Broad Business Value Through Advanced Enterprise Performance Management' (2011). www.accenture.com/us-en/Pages/service-advanced-enterprise-performance-management-summary.aspx; accessed 14 February 2011.

26 Accenture, 'Accenture Advanced Enterprise Performance Management Solution for SAP' (2009). Pdf published online at www.accenture.com/SiteCollectionDocuments/PDF/AEPM_for_SAP_Print_Brochure_FINAL_3309.pdf; accessed 13 February 2011.

27 Krangel, E., 'SAP: Clueless Consultants from Accenture and IBM Giving Us a Bad Name (SAP)' (2009). Business Insider. www.businessinsider.com/2009/2/sap-clueless-consultants-from-accenture-and-ibm-giving-us-a-bad-name-sap. Accessed 14 February 2011.

28 White, R. and Schotter, A., *Jacques Kemp: Towards Performance Excellence*, London, Ontario: Ivey Publishing, 2006.

29 Harvard Business School Case 906M83.

30 Warner, M. and Witzel, M., *Managing in Virtual Organizations*, London: International Thomson Business Press, 2004.

3 Planning for fameworks

1 'NHS Told to Abandon Delayed IT Project', *Guardian*, 22 September 2011.

2 Bennis, Warren G. and Nanus, Bert, *Leaders: Five Strategies for Taking Charge*, New York: Harper & Row, 1985.

3 Collins and Porras, *Built to Last*.
4 See for example Collins and Porras, *Built to Last*; Barwise, P. and Meehan, S., *Beyond the Familiar: Long-Term Growth Through Customer Focus and Innovation*, San Francisco: Jossey-Bass, 2011.
5 Collins, *Good to Great: Why some Companies Make the Leap . . . and others don't*, New York: Harper Business, 2001.
6 See for example Andrews, K. R., *The Concept of Corporate Strategy*, Homewood, IL: Irwin; Mintzberg, *The Rise and Fall of Strategic Planning*; and for an overview of the different schools, the introduction to McKiernan, P. (ed.), *Historical Evolution of Strategic Management*, Aldershot: Dartmouth, 1996.
7 *Financial Times*, 14 June 2011.
8 Barwise and Meehan, *Beyond the Familiar*.
9 Fuerst, M. and Schotter, A., 'Strategic Compliance and Integrity Management: A Mission Critical Dynamic Capability', in T. Wilkinson and A. Thomas, *Strategic Management in the 21st Century*, Westport, CT: Praeger, forthcoming, 2013.
10 Kaplan and Norton, *The Balanced Scorecard*.
11 Hrebiniak, Lawrence G., *Making Strategy Work: Leading Effective Execution and Change*, Upper Saddle River, NJ: Wharton School Publishing, 2008, p. 3.

4 The portfolio driver

1 Zook, Chris, *Unstoppable: Finding Hidden Assets to Review the Core and Fuel Profitable Growth*, Boston: Harvard Business School Press, 2007.
2 Chakravarthy, B. and Lorange, P. *Profit or Growth: Why You Don't Have to Choose*.
3 Straub, T., *Reasons for Frequent Failure in Mergers and Acquistions: A Comprehensive Analysis*.
4 Witzel, M., *Tata: The Evolution of a Corporate Brand*.

5 The marketing driver

1 Drucker, *The Practice of Management*.
2 Theodore Levitt, 'Marketing Myopia', *Harvard Business Review*, 53(5) (1975): 10.
3 Tim Ambler, *Marketing and the Bottom Line*, p. 1.
4 Kotler, *Marketing Management*.
5 Aaker, David A. (1992) *Managing Brand Equity: Capitalizing on the Power of a Brand Name*, New York: The Free Press; Hatch, Mary Jo and Schultz, Majken, *Taking Brand Initiative: How Companies Can Align Strategy, Culture and Identity Through Corporate Branding*, Chichester: John Wiley, 2008.
6 Kim, W. Chan and Mauborgne, Renée, *Blue Ocean Strategy: How to Create Uncontested Market Space and Make the Competition Irrelevant*, Boston: Harvard Business School Press, 2005.
7 Hofstede, Geert, *Cultures and Organizations: Software of the Mind*, London: McGraw-Hill, 1991.
8 Maslow, Abraham, *Motivation and Personality*, New York: Harper & Bros, 1954.

9 Bijapurkar, Rama, *We Are Like That Only*, New Delhi: Penguin India, 2007.
10 Bateson and Hoffman, *Managing Services Marketing*.
11 Barwise and Meehan, *Beyond the Familiar*.
12 Barwise and Meehan, *Beyond the Familiar*.
13 W. Chan Kim and Renée Mauborgne, *Blue Ocean Strategy*.
14 Collins and Rustad, 'Can You Say What Your Strategy Is?.'
15 Hatch and Schultz, *Taking Brand Initiative*.

6 The organizational driver

1 Peters and Waterman, *In Search of Excellence*.
2 Erdal, David, 'Beyond the Corporation: Humanity Working', *Financial Times*, 21–22 January 2011.
3 Hope, Jeremy, *Reinventing the CFO*, Boston: Harvard Business School Press, 1996.
4 Chandler, *Strategy and Structure*.
5 Collins and Porras, *Built to Last*.
6 Miles, Raymond E. and Snow, Charles C., *Organizational Strategy, Structure and Process*, New York: McGraw-Hill, 1978.
7 Porter, *Competitive Strategy*.
8 'Inside Nokia', *Financial Times*, 14 April 2011.
9 Interviewed in *The Smart Manager*, 2006.
10 See Bolden *et al.*, *Exploring Leadership*.
11 Nonaka and Takeuchi, *The Knowledge-Creating Company*.

7 The operational driver

1 Crosby, *Quality is Free*.
2 Grove, *Only the Paranoid Survive*.

8 The reputation driver

1 Hatch and Schultz, *Taking Brand Initiative*.
2 Witzel, *Tata: The Evolution of a Corporate Brand*.
3 Ibid.
4 Siedel, *Using the Law for Competitive Advantage*.
5 Sharpe Paine, 'Managing Organizational Integrity'.
6 Jennings, *The Seven Signs of Ethical Collapse*.
7 Fuerst, M. and Schotter, A., 'Strategic Compliance and Integrity Management: A Mission Critical Dynamic Capability', in T. Wilkinson and A. Thomas, *Strategic Management in the 21st Century*, Westport, CT: Praeger, forthcoming, 2013.

9 The financial driver

1 Chakravarthy and Lorange, *Profit or Growth*; Samuel C. Weaver, *The Essentials of Financial Analysis*, New York: McGraw-Hill, 2012; John J. Hampton, *The AMA Handbook of Financial Risk Management*, New York: Amacom, 2011.

2 Shiller, Robert J., *Irrational Exuberance*, New York: Crown Press, 2001.
3 Hope, *Reinventing the CFO*.
4 Hope, *Reinventing the CFO*.
5 *Financial Times*, 6 June 2010.

10 Performance excellence

1 *Financial Times*, 18 April 2011.

11 Connecting the dots

1 *Financial Times*, 30 September 2009.
2 *McKinsey Quarterly*, 24 October 2007.

BIBLIOGRAPHY

Aaker, David A. (1992) *Managing Brand Equity: Capitalizing on the Power of a Brand Name*, New York: The Free Press.

Ambler, Tim (2000) *Marketing and the Bottom Line: The New Metrics of Corporate Wealth*, London: FT/Prentice Hall.

Andersen, Michael Moesgaard, Froholdt, Morten and Poulfelt, Flemming (2010) *Return on Strategy: How to Achieve It*, New York: T&F books.

Andrews, Kenneth R. (1971) *The Concept of Corporate Strategy*, Homewood, IL: Irwin.

Ansoff, H. Igor (1965) *Corporate Strategy*, London: McGraw-Hill.

Barwise, Patrick and Meehan, Seán (2011) *Beyond the Familiar: Long-Term Growth Through Customer Focus and Innovation*, San Francisco: Jossey-Bass.

Bateson, J. E. G. and Hoffman, K. D. (1999) *Managing Services Marketing*, Dallas: South-Western.

Beinhocker, Eric D. (2007) *The Origin of Wealth: Evolution, Complexity and the Radical Remaking of Economics*, New York: Random House.

Bennis, Warren G. and Nanus, Bert (1985) *Leaders: Five Strategies for Taking Charge*, New York: Harper & Row.

Bijapurkar, Rama (2007) *We Are Like That Only*, New Delhi: Penguin India.

Bolden, Richard, Hawkins, Beverly, Gosling, Jonathan and Taylor, Scott (2011) *Exploring Leadership: Individual, Organizational and Social Perspectives*, Oxford: Oxford University Press.

Casson, Herbert N. (1931) *The Story of My Life*, London: Efficiency Magazine.

Chakravarthy, Bala and Lorange, Peter (2007) *Profit or Growth: Why You Don't Have to Choose*, Engelwood Cliffs, NJ: Prentice Hall.

Chandler, Alfred D. (1962) *Strategy and Structure: Chapters in the History of American Industrial Enterprise*, Cambridge, MA: MIT Press.

— (1977) *The Visible Hand: The Managerial Revolution in American Business*, Cambridge, MA: Belknap Press.

Chapman, Peter (2010) *The Last of the Imperious Rich: Lehman Brothers, 1844–2008*, London: Portfolio.

Coelho, A. and Purdy, L. (2003) *Two Alternative Approaches to the Evaluation of Performance: 360-Degree Feedback and the Balanced Scorecard*, London, Ontario: Ivey Publishing.

Collins, James (2001) *Good to Great: Why Some Companies Make the Leap . . . And Others Don't*, New York: HarperBusiness.

—— and Hansen, Morten (2011) *Great by Choice*, New York: HarperBusiness.

—— and Porras, Jerry (1997) *Built to Last: The Successful Habits of Visionary Companies*, New York: HarperBusiness.

Collis, David J. and Rukstad, Michael G. (2008) 'Can You Say What Your Strategy Is?', *Harvard Business Review*, 7(4): 1–10.

Crosby, Philip (1979) *Quality Is Free: The Art of Making Quality Certain*, New York: McGraw-Hill.

Drucker, Peter F. (1954) *The Practice of Management*, New York: Harper & Row.

Erdal, David (2011) 'Beyond the Corporation: Humanity Working', *Financial Times*, 21–22 January.

Fayol, Henri (1916) *Administration industrielle et générale*, trans. Irwin Gray, New York: David S. Lake, 1984.

Fitzgerald, Tom and Collins, John (2006) 'The CFO as Corporate Prophet', *Corporate Finance Review*, 3 (July–August): 1–10.

Fuerst, M. and Schotter, A. (2013, forthcoming) 'Strategic Compliance and Integrity Management: A Mission Critical Dynamic Capability', in T. Wilkinson and A. Thomas, *Strategic Management in the 21st Century*, Westport, CT: Praeger.

Gordon, Robert J. (1990) *The American Business Cycle: Continuity and Change*, Chicago: University of Chicago Press.

Greto, M., Schotter, A. and Teagarden, M. (2010) *Toyota: The Accelerator Crisis*, Thunderbird Case Series. Glendale, AZ: Thunderbird School of Global Management.

Grove, Andrew (1996) *Only the Paranoid Survive: How to Exploit the Crisis Points that Challenge Every Company and Career*, New York: HarperCollins.

Gulick, Luther H. (1937) 'Notes on the Theory of Organization', in Luther H. Gulick and Lyndall Urwick (eds), *Papers on the Science of Administration*, New York: Institute for Public Administration.

Hampton, John J. (2011) *The AMA Handbook of Financial Risk Management*, New York: Amacom.

Handy, Charles (1995) *The Empty Raincoat*, London: Arrow.

Hatch, Mary Jo and Schultz, Majken (2008) *Taking Brand Initiative: How Companies Can Align Strategy, Culture and Identity Through Corporate Branding*, Chichester: John Wiley.

Hofstede, Geert (1991) *Cultures and Organizations: Software of the Mind*, London: McGraw-Hill.

Hope, Jeremy (1996) *Reinventing the CFO*, Boston: Harvard Business School Press.

—— and Player, Steve (2012) *Beyond Performance Management*, Boston: Harvard Business School Press.

Hrebiniak, Lawrence G. (2008) *Making Strategy Work: Leading Effective Execution and Change*, Upper Saddle River, NJ: Wharton School Publishing, p. 3.

Jennings, M. (2006) *The Seven Signs of Ethical Collapse: How to Spot Moral Meltdowns in Companies . . . Before It's Too Late*, New York: St. Martin's Press.

Kahneman, Daniel (2011) *Thinking Fast and Slow*, New York: Farrar, Straus and Giroux.

Kanigel, Robert (1997) *The One Best Way: Frederick Taylor and the Enigma of Efficiency*, New York: Viking Penguin.

Kaplan, R. and Norton, D. (1992) 'The Balanced Scorecard: Measures That Drive Performance', *Harvard Business Review*, 69(1): 71–79.

—— (1996a) *The Balanced Scorecard: Translating Strategy into Action*, Boston: Harvard Business School Press.

—— (1996b) 'Linking the Balanced Scorecard to Strategy', *California Management Review*, 39(1): 53–79.

Kaplan, R. and Norton, D. (2000) 'Having Trouble with Your Strategy? Then Map It', *Harvard Business Review*, 77: 167–76.

—— (2001) *The Strategy Focused Organization*, Boston: Harvard Business School Press.

Kay, John (2010) *Obliquity: Why Our Goals Are Best Achieved Indirectly*, London: Profile Books.

Kim, W. Chan and Mauborgne, Renée (2005) *Blue Ocean Strategy: How to Create Uncontested Market Space and Make the Competition Irrelevant*, Boston: Harvard Business School Press.

Kotler, Philip (1997) *Marketing Management*, Engelwood Cliffs, NJ: Prentice-Hall, 9th edn.

Levitt, Theodore (1960) 'Marketing Myopia', *Harvard Business Review*, 38(4): 45–56; reprinted with a retrospective commentary, *Harvard Business Review*, 53(5) (1975): 1–14.

Maslow, Abraham (1954) *Motivation and Personality*, New York: Harper & Bros.

McKiernan, Peter (ed.) (1996) *Historical Evolution of Strategic Management*, Aldershot: Dartmouth, 2 vols.

Miles, Raymond E. and Snow, Charles C. (1978) *Organizational Strategy, Structure and Process*, New York: McGraw-Hill.

Mintzberg, Henry (1989) *Mintzberg on Management*, New York: The Free Press.

—— (1994) *The Rise and Fall of Strategic Planning*, New York: The Free Press.

Nonaka, Ikujiro and Takeuchi, Hirotaka (1995) *The Knowledge-Creating Company: How Japanese Companies Create the Dynamics of Innovation*, Oxford: Oxford University Press.

Peters, T. and Waterman, R. (1982) *In Search of Excellence*, New York and London: Harper & Row.

Porter, Michael E. (1980) *Competitive Strategy: Techniques for Analyzing Industries and Competitors*, New York: The Free Press.

Pryor, Mildred Golden, White, J. Chris and Toombs, Leslie A. (1998) *Strategic Quality Management: A Strategic, Systems Approach to Quality*. New York: Thomson Learning.

Pryor, M. G., Anderson, D., Toombs, L. A. and Humphreys, J. H. (2007) 'Strategic Implementation as a Core Competency: The 5P's model', *Journal of Management Research*, 7(1): 3–17.

Rasiel, E. and Friga, P. N. (2001) *The McKinsey Mind: Understanding and Implementing the Problem-Solving Tools and Management Techniques of the World's Top Strategic Consulting Firm*, New York: McGraw-Hill.

Richardson, Kurt (2008) 'Managing Complex Organizations: Complexity Thinking and the Science and Art of Management', *Corporate Finance Review*, 10(2): (2008) 13–26.

Schotter, A. and Beamish, P. W. (2011) 'Performance Effects of MNC Headquarters – Subsidiary Conflict and the Role of Boundary Spanners: The Case of Headquarter Initiative Rejection', *Journal of International Management*, 17(3): 243–59.

Schotter, Andreas, Beamish, Paul W. and White, Rod (2007) *ING Insurance Asia/ Pacific*, London, Ontario: Ivey Publishing.

Sharpe Paine, L. (1994) 'Managing Organizational Integrity', *Harvard Business Review*, 72(2): 106–17.

Sheth, Jagdish (2007) *The Self-Destructive Habits of Good Companies*, Upper Saddle River, NJ: Wharton School Publishing.

Shiller, Robert J. (2001) *Irrational Exuberance*, New York: Broadway.

Siedel, George (2002) *Using the Law for Competitive Advantage*, San Francisco: Jossey-Bass.

David J. Snowden and Mary E. Boone (2007) 'A Leader's Framework for Decision Making', *Harvard Business Review*, November: 69–76.

Spencer, Herbert (1864) *Principles of Biology*, London; repr. Honolulu, University Press of the Pacific, 1962.

Straub, Thomas (2007) *Reasons for Frequent Failure in Mergers and Acquisitions: A Comprehensive Analysis*, Wiesbaden, Germany: Deutscher Universitäts-Verlag.

Taylor, Frederick Winslow (1911) *The Principles of Scientific Management*, New York: Harper & Bros.

Warner, Malcolm and Witzel, Morgen (2004) *Managing in Virtual Organizations*, London: International Thomson Business Press.

Weaver, Samuel C. (2012) *The Essentials of Financial Analysis*, New York: McGraw-Hill.

White, R. and Schotter, A. (2006) *Jacques Kemp: Towards Performance Excellence*, London, Ontario: Ivey Publishing. Case no. 9B06M084.

Witzel, Morgen (2010) *Tata: The Evolution of a Corporate Brand*, New Delhi: Penguin Portfolio.

Zook, Chris, (2007) *Unstoppable: Finding Hidden Assets to Review the Core and Fuel Profitable Growth*, Boston: Harvard Business School Press, .

INDEX